CAMPAIGN 402

BLOOD RIVER 1838

The Zulu–Boer War and the Great Trek

IAN KNIGHT

ILLUSTRATED BY ADAM HOOK

OSPREY PUBLISHING
Bloomsbury Publishing Plc
Kemp House, Chawley Park, Cumnor Hill, Oxford OX2 9PH, UK
29 Earlsfort Terrace, Dublin 2, Ireland
1385 Broadway, 5th Floor, New York, NY 10018, USA
E-mail: info@ospreypublishing.com
www.ospreypublishing.com

OSPREY is a trademark of Osprey Publishing Ltd

First published in Great Britain in 2024

A catalogue record for this book is available from the British Library.

ISBN: PB 9781472860750; eBook 9781472860743;
ePDF 9781472860736; XML 9781472860767

24 25 26 27 28 10 9 8 7 6 5 4 3 2 1

Maps by Bounford.com
3D BEVs by Paul Kime
Index by Zoe Ross
Typeset by PDQ Digital Media Solutions, Bungay, UK
Printed by Repro India Ltd.

MIX
Paper
FSC FSC® C047271

Artist's note

Readers may care to note that the original paintings from which the colour plates in this book were prepared are available for private sale. All reproduction copyright whatsoever is retained by the publishers. All enquiries should be addressed to:

Scorpio, 158 Mill Road, Hailsham, East Sussex BN27 2SH, UK
Email: scorpiopaintings@btinternet.com

The publishers regret that they can enter into no correspondence upon this matter.

Osprey Publishing supports the Woodland Trust, the UK's leading woodland conservation charity.

To find out more about our authors and books visit **www.ospreypublishing.com**. Here you will find extracts, author interviews, details of forthcoming events and the option to sign up for our newsletter.

Front cover main illustration: A fresh Zulu regiment crossing the *donga* and approaching the Boer *laager* during the battle of Blood River/Ncome. (Adam Hook)
Title page image: The modern-day view towards the wagon *laager* on the bank of the Ncome River. (Author)

CONTENTS

ORIGINS OF THE CAMPAIGN

Late on the afternoon of 23 September 1828, the great Zulu king, Shaka kaSenzangakhona, was assassinated in a palace coup. His killers were two of his brothers, the princes Dingane and Mhlangana, who, with the covert help of King Shaka's trusted aunt, Mnkabayi, had laid their plot carefully. King Shaka had been a strong leader who had forged the Zulu kingdom over a period of 12 years by an adroit mix of astute diplomacy and ruthless military force, expanding from a small heartland by incorporating neighbouring groups with various degrees of coercion and persuasion. By 1827, however, the strain of managing the kingdom, imposing new unifying administrative structures, containing internal dissent and countering external threats was beginning to tell, and King Shaka's behaviour had become increasingly erratic. Sensing that the public mood within the kingdom was leaving the king increasingly isolated, the two princes had waited until Shaka's army was away on campaign, and had surprised him as he was sitting outside his hut in a small private enclave outside his great royal homestead at KwaDukuza, accompanied by only a handful of courtiers and envoys. The assassins had been able to surprise him and stab him to death. However, according to Zulu tradition, as he lay dying, Shaka had admonished his killers, predicting that the Zulu Royal House would ruin itself through fratricidal in-fighting, and that as a result the country would fall prey to Europeans, who were coming like locusts to eat it up.

By the end of the 18th century, the farming community, the descendants of the original Dutch and French Huguenot settlers at the Cape, had begun to develop a distinct identity and lived hardy lives largely dependent on their own self-reliance. (Author)

Shaka's last words would undoubtedly accrue extra weight among the Zulu people as the century wore on. Europeans were a new phenomenon in Zululand in the 1820s; they had only arrived there in 1824, just four years before Shaka's death, yet they represented a spearhead of powerful forces and movements generated far beyond Zululand, over which the Zulus had no control, but which would quickly bring them into the first of a series of conflicts that would ultimately lead to the loss of the kingdom's independence.

The coming of the British. Lt Gen. Jan Willem Janssens attempts to rally his wavering troops in this romanticized image of the battle of Blaauberg on 8 January 1806. The defeat of Janssens' Batavian troops in a conventional battle on the sand dunes opposite Cape Town saw control of the Cape pass from the Dutch to the British. (Author)

The first European settlement in southern Africa was established by the Dutch East India Company (*Verenigde Oost-Indische Compagnie*) in the 17th century, a tiny enclave at the foot of Table Mountain, at the very tip of the continent, which was built to provision Dutch ships on the long maritime haul from Europe to their colonies in Indonesia. The Dutch had little interest in the African hinterland, but established a small colony of farmers and artisans, many of them Protestant refugees from religious conflicts in Europe, who, over the following century, developed an independent spirit and self-reliant lifestyle on the frontiers of the colony. They were known by the Dutch word for country-folk – *boere*, commonly given as Boer – and spoke a version of Dutch blended with the local Khoekhoe and San languages, and influenced by Indonesian words that were imported with the slaves the Dutch administration brought from its eastern colonies. Religiously devout, they were geographically separated and intellectually isolated from currents of mainstream thought in Europe, and gradually began to think of themselves as a distinct people.

The need for new pastures imparted an expansionist dynamic of the eastern frontier of the Cape Colony, which brought them into conflict with robust African societies beyond the colony's borders, notably the amaXhosa people in the fertile downlands on the eastern coastal seaboard. This tension was already established before ownership of the Cape Colony passed dramatically from the control of the Dutch to the British at the beginning of the 19th century. For the British, interest in the Cape reflected the wider strategic interests in their own empire and was a result of their international rivalry with France. The dramatic twists and turns that followed the collapse of the monarchy in France and the rise of Napoleon Bonaparte, and in particular the growth of French influence over the Netherlands, raised for the British the spectre that control of the Cape might pass to an overtly hostile power, and that this might threaten Britain's lines of communication with its own Indian empire. In 1806, a British amphibious expedition defeated pro-French Dutch forces at the battle of Blaauberg, on the sandy beaches opposite Table Mountain, and the British took control of the Cape. While much of the colony acquiesced in the transition, the arrival of the British was widely resented among the Boer communities on the Eastern Cape, who were used to living a life largely without interference from Cape Town and who considered that their survival offered particular challenges that the British

A patrol of burghers is surrounded during the Sixth Eastern Cape Frontier War (1834–35). The illustration shows how vulnerable burghers could be away from their horses, and gives a good impression of Boer dress of the period. Disillusion among the frontier community at the inability of British troops to protect them in this war was a significant factor in the emergence of the Trek movement. (Author)

failed to understand. British rule brought with it a more metropolitan and liberal world view, which seemed less supportive of the rural communities in their disputes with both African neighbours and their own farm workers, and which seemed to challenge many of the ideological props of Boer life. For the most part, the British were no more interested in expanding territorial claims into the interior than the Dutch had been, but with the defeat of Napoleon at Waterloo in 1815, the British were free from their long-standing struggle against France and were able to expand their imperial aspirations unchecked around the world. In 1820, in an attempt to bolster European settlement along the contested Eastern Cape frontier, the British had sponsored a new settlement scheme from home, which added a further complicating factor to the fragile politics of the region.

It was as a by-product of this growing British presence in southern Africa that the first direct contact was made between them and the Zulu kingdom. In 1824, a consortium of Cape merchants commissioned a small party of predominantly British traders and hunters to sail up the eastern coast, beyond the colony's boundaries, and make the dangerous crossing over a treacherous sandbar into a sheltered bay known as the Bay of Natal. Here,

The frustration with the perceived unsympathetic nature of British rule led to a wholesale exodus from the Cape frontier regions from 1837. Here, Trekker parties cross the open grasslands north of the Senqu (Orange) River. (Author)

the traders established a ramshackle camp within the southern orbit of the Zulu kingdom and established contact with King Shaka. Shaka, recognizing the value of the access to exotic foreign goods they afforded him, offered his protection to the settlement, trading cattle and ivory in return for beads, blankets and the occasional military service of the traders.

As the optimistically named Port Natal settlement slowly grew, however, so the relationship between the British administration at the Cape and the frontier farmers continued to deteriorate. Long used to managing their affairs with a minimum of governmental interference, and bolstered by a robust Calvinist faith and an ingrained sense of cultural and racial superiority, the frontier Boers were unsettled by the imposition of English as the colony's official language and by an apparent even-handedness in dealing with disputes between farmers and indigenous communities. In 1833, the British had abolished slavery within their overseas possessions, and this came into effect at the Cape in December 1834. There were over 40,000 enslaved people within the colony, many of them descended from the Indonesian population imported by the Dutch, and the process by which the farmers were compensated for the loss of the value of their 'property' could be cumbersome. In reality, only a few wealthy families on the remote frontier were heavily dependent upon slave labour, but the process was seen by many there as indicative of unsympathetic attitudes and an attack on the perceived natural order.

By the middle of 1834, some more adventurous frontier farmers had already begun to think that their future lay in removing themselves from the boundaries of British influence and seeking out new lands where they could govern themselves according to their own needs and beliefs. Several small expeditions were quietly sent into the interior to investigate the political and physical terrain there, and they had scarcely returned when a fresh war broke out on the frontier – the sixth in a cycle of nine, which encompassed almost exactly a century. Both the frontier community and the amaXhosa were cattle-owning societies who competed for access to the best grazing lands, and friction between them was common. The wounding of a Xhosa chief in a minor skirmish led to a Xhosa invasion of the frontier at the end of 1834, which destroyed farms and carried away the livestock of Boer and '1820 settlers' alike. Although the Xhosa were eventually defeated, many Boers were convinced that the British lacked both the ability and the will to protect them, and the losses stimulated the impetus to abandon the colony altogether.

Once the Great Trek began in earnest, the Trekkers faced an array of formidable natural obstacles, moving their ox-wagons across them from steep mountain passes to wide rivers. (Author)

The resulting movement is known as the Great Trek, although the title implies more sense of unity and purpose than it actually possessed. It was in fact a series of pulses in emigration in which communities, often linked by ties of family or patronage, packed their possessions into their ox-wagons and, accompanied by their African workers and driving their herds of cattle and flocks of sheep with them, crossed the boundaries of the colony, often with no clear sense of objective beyond placing themselves out of reach of British jurisdiction. Between 1836 and 1838, some 8,000 Boers, including women and children, left the colony, taking with them half as many of their African dependants as labourers, servants, herdsmen and wagon drivers. By their nature independent-minded, these parties of Trekkers sometimes came together to pursue a common goal, but just as often fragmented, their patriarchs unwilling to bind themselves too closely to the aspirations or prestige of others. For the most part avoiding the densely populated Eastern frontier, they headed north instead, separated from the coastal strip by the great chain of the uKhahlamba mountains – which they called the Drakensberg, the 'Dragon Mountains' – and moved through the more open grass uplands of the highveld. Some began to settle once they had crossed the Sangqu (Orange) River, while the more determined continued north across the Lekwa River, which they called the Vaal. They managed to avoid outright conflict with the Sotho people in the south, but further north clashed violently with the amaNdebele kingdom, which had itself been formed along Zulu lines by refugees fleeing King Shaka's rise on the coast. The Boer–Ndebele campaign of 1836–37 demonstrated both the vulnerability of scattered and disunited Boer groups, and their strengths when combining together to rely on their firepower, horses and the defensive capabilities of their wagons. The Ndebele kingdom was driven out, paving

A Boer family and their African servant on trek. During the exodus of the 1830s the ox-wagon became both a mobile home and a means of defence. (Author)

The battle of Vegkop, October 1836 – the defining battle between the Trekkers and the amaNdebele kingdom of King Mzilikazi kaMashobane. A series of unsuccessful Ndebele attacks on a defensive circle of wagons demonstrated the effectiveness of a wagon fortification against even the most determined attackers. (Author)

the way for the emergence of an independent Boer state. The Trekkers would go on to form a number of settlements, and while these, too, would rise and fall, fragment and coalesce, two main independent republics would endure: the Orange Free State to the south and the Transvaal to the north.

The Zulus were well aware of the fortunes of the amaNdebele kingdom, with whom they had their own disputes, and news of their defeat filtered through to them. The decade since King Shaka's assassination had been spent in consolidation; in the immediate aftermath, Prince Dingane had eliminated his co-conspirator and been installed as king. In an effort to contain the political fallout from the coup, and to quell internal opposition, he had moved the centre of his kingdom north, back to the old Zulu heartland, and established his new royal homestead at eMgungundlovu in the open valley of the Mhkumbane stream south of the White Mfolozi River. This had effectively loosened Zulu control over the African groups in what had been the southern part of Shaka's kingdom, across the Thukela River, and had allowed the small settler community at Port Natal a new degree of autonomy and influence.

While many of the Trekker groups were content to exploit their recent conquest of the interior, at least one, led by an Eastern Cape farmer named Piet Retief, saw possibilities in Natal. The country was rich and fertile, but it was far more densely populated than any the Trekkers had hitherto encountered, the military might of the Zulus was greater than that of the Ndebele and the presence of British traders on

Defending a wagon *laager*. This illustration stresses how important the *laager* was when family groups were attacked, and the role played by Trekker women in loading guns for the defenders. In fact, the Trekkers fought from behind the wagon barricade, and any who exposed themselves like this on top of the wagons would have been very vulnerable to thrown spears. (Author)

King Dingane kaSenzangakhona – eyewitness impressions by a missionary, Captain Allen Gardiner. Gardiner's surprisingly jaunty sketches capture the king in a variety of costumes but fail to reflect his elusive, secretive and ultimately self-destructive personality. (Author)

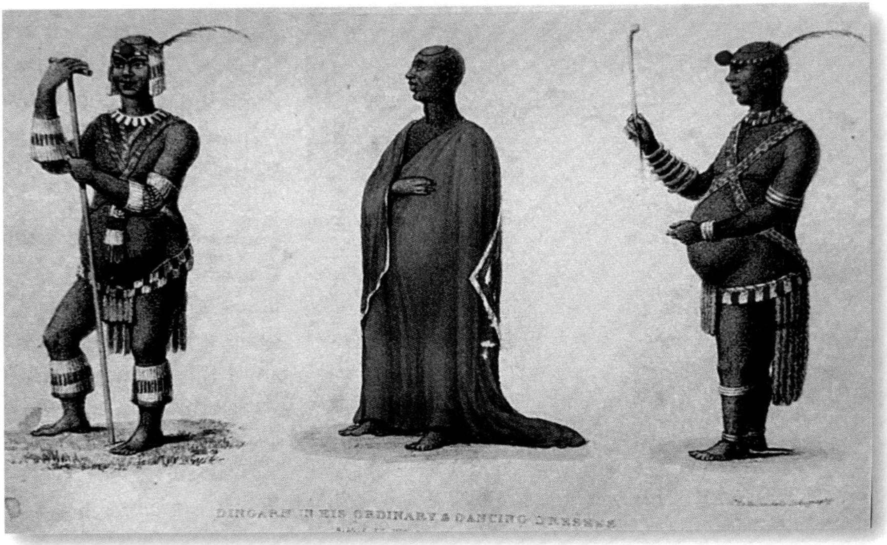

the coast implied a connection with British authority beyond. Retief, however, saw an opportunity in the uncertain authority south of the Thukela, and in September 1837 he brought his own followers to the western side of the uKhahlamba mountains before he crossed the dangerous mountain passes and made his way to Port Natal with a small party of just 15 men. Having reassured himself that the traders there were essentially sympathetic, he made his way to eMgungundlovu to seek permission from King Dingane to settle his party south of the Thukela.

King Dingane was well aware that the Trekkers were very different to the Port Natal settlers, who sought to trade and hunt, but had no great hunger for land; the Boers, like the Zulus, were pastoralists and their great herds were testimony to their need for land. King Dingane had survived at his predecessor's court and successfully staged Shaka's assassination through his ability to mask his thoughts and intentions, and whilst he therefore regarded Retief with suspicion, he nonetheless received the Boer envoy courteously. Retief was already full of confidence that his leadership was bolstered by divine support, and he reacted to the king's apparent

King Dingane's eMgungundlovu royal homestead, the greatest of the Zulu *amakhanda*, which served as barracks for the Zulu army and for the dissemination of royal authority. Widely regarded as the greatest of the 19th-century Zulu palaces, eMgungundlovu was the site of King Dingane's meetings with Piet Retief. (Author)

friendliness with a tone that swung between the arrogant and the cajoling. Over the next three months, he would blunder badly in his dealings with King Dingane, unwittingly reinforcing the Zulu wariness of Trekker intentions. Nevertheless, King Dingane agreed to the possibility of granting the Trekkers the right to settle but remained vague as to where, offering to discuss this further should Retief demonstrate his good faith by carrying out a commission on Dingane's behalf. Two years earlier, cattle belonging to a group under Zulu protection had been stolen by a Sotho clan, the Batlokwa of King Sekonyela, who lived across the uKhahlamba mountains. Sekonyela had haughtily refused Zulu demands to return them, and Dingane saw in Retief a means of both recovering his cattle and testing the Trekkers' sincerity.

Piet Retief, a farmer from the Graaff-Reinet district of the Eastern Cape, was the one Trek leader who was determined to settle in the lush pastures of Natal. His miscalculations in his dealings with the Zulu King Dingane would, however, lead to a bloody outcome which precipitated the most desperate conflict fought during the Great Trek. (Author)

Retief, delighted with his apparent success, immediately sent word to his followers waiting beyond the mountain passes. In the middle of November 1837, convinced that they had finally found the chosen land to which their God had been leading them, the Trekkers began the steep and dangerous descent of the uKhahlamba and spilled out onto the rolling country along the Mtshezi River, which they rechristened the Boesmansrivier – Bushmans River – and the Msuluzi River, which they called the Bloukrans. The area was thinly populated and the inhabitants abandoned their homes before them, allowing the Trekkers to collect wagonloads of grain. By the end of November, as many as a thousand wagons were clustered in family camps across the mountain foothills.

All of this was far in advance of the agreement reached between King Dingane and Piet Retief. Nevertheless, at the end of December, Retief assembled a *kommando* – an armed force of Boers – and made his way to Sekonyela. Here, Retief persuaded Sekonyela to meet him – and in a dramatic moment snapped handcuffs on the unsuspecting king's wrists. Frightened for his life, Sekonyela agreed to give up the cattle demanded by King Dingane. Retief, delighted by his success, promptly sent news to Dingane – but the Zulu king reacted very differently to the way in which Retief had hoped. Uneasy at the way in which Retief had treated a fellow king – could he then be trusted in his dealings with the Zulu? – and disturbed by Retief's apparent determination to keep part of the recaptured booty as a commission, King Dingane became yet more firmly convinced of the Trekkers' insincerity.

THE OUTBREAK OF WAR

Retief set out at the end of January to complete his negotiations with the Zulu king. This time he was accompanied by 69 burghers and 30 mixed-race servants and grooms – known as *agterryers* – and was determined

King Dingane reclines in his hut, surrounded by the female attendants of his *isigodlo*, his personal household. At the time of the Trekker intrusion, the Zulu kingdom was the most powerful independent African kingdom in southern Africa. (Author)

to follow up his success over Sekonyela by impressing Dingane with their military prowess.

The Trekkers arrived at eMgungundlovu on 3 February 1838 to find that several of the Zulu *amabutho* – regiments – had already assembled for the occasion. For three days, the Trekkers were entertained at the royal homestead while Retief and the king reached an agreement which would

A frieze on the Voortrekker Monument in Pretoria conflates the two elements of the interaction between King Dingane and Piet Retief: the signing of the concession granting land in Natal to the Trekkers, and the murder of Retief and his entre party. (Anagoria via Wikimedia Commons, CC BY 3.0)

A view of eMgungundlovu, showing the dramatic moment on 6 February 1838 when, at King Dingane's direction, the assembled Zulu *amabutho* seized Piet Retief, his companions and their *agterryers*, and dragged them away to their deaths. (Author)

cede the area south of the Thukela River, including the Port Natal settlement, to the Boers. Retief's men celebrated by firing their muskets in a show of strength, while the Zulu *amabutho* took part in complex dances.

However, the celebrations were premature. Worried by stories of the ease with which the Trekkers had driven the Ndebele kingdom out of the highveld, and suspicious of Retief's treatment of Sekonyela, King Dingane had convinced himself that the Trekkers would be dangerous neighbours – and had determined to take extreme action to remove the threat. Early on the morning of 6 February, he agreed to meet the Trekkers for one farewell celebration before they returned to their encampments. It was considered bad manners to carry weapons in the presence of the king, and the Trekkers were instructed to leave their muskets at the entrance to the homestead. Several thousand warriors were drawn up within the enclosure, carrying shields and dancing sticks. The *amabutho* began to dance, advancing and retreating towards the seated Boers, until Dingane suddenly called out 'Seize them!' Although a few of the Trekkers attempted to put up a fight with their knives or fists, they were quickly overpowered, and as they were dragged away through the main entrance of eMgungundlovu, Dingane called out '*Bulaleni abathakathi!*' – 'Kill the wizards!' The helpless Trekkers were dragged off to the nearby hill of execution, KwaMatiwane, where Zulu criminals were put to death, and killed with the warriors' dancing sticks. Only one of the *agterryers*, who had been

'Seize them!' At King Dingane's command, Retief and his party are overwhelmed and carried to KwaMatiwane, the hill of execution. The king's attempt to remove the Trekker threat in a single blow failed, however, and provoked two years of bitter warfare. (Author)

The Boer–Zulu War, February–April 1838

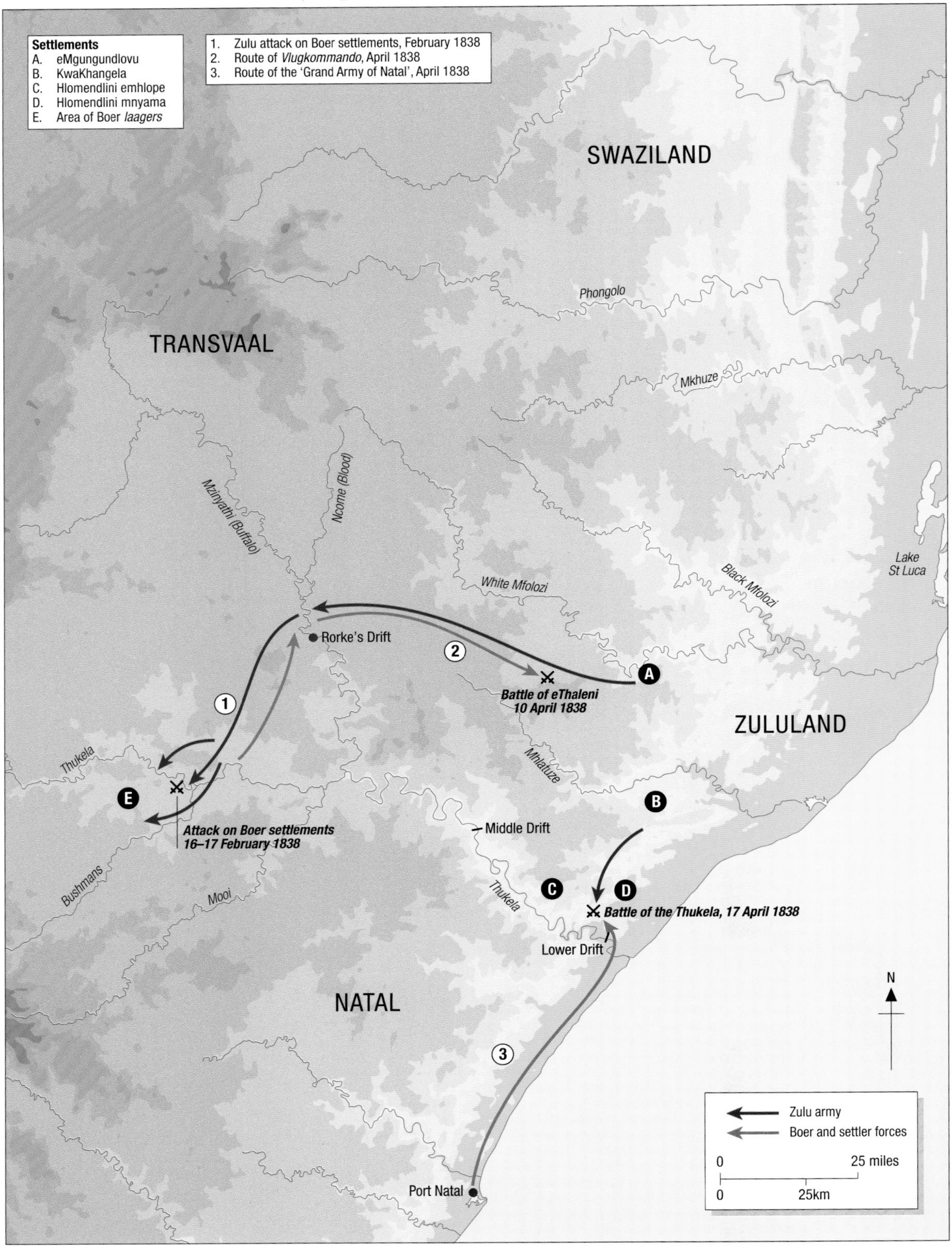

The site of eMgungundlovu today; the view is from the hill of execution, KwaMatiwane, with the Piet Retief monument in the foreground, looking across to the royal homestead, which occupied the cleared area on the slope beyond. (Author)

looking after the party's horses by the gate, managed to escape – Retief and all his followers were killed.

In Zulu law, the lives of the families of a wrongdoer were considered tainted by association and were forfeit; and in any case, Dingane was well aware that the Trekker encampments scattered across the uKhahlamba foothills afforded a springboard for retaliation. No sooner were Retief and his men dead, than Dingane despatched several *amabutho* to attack the Boer encampments. It took the *amabutho* about ten days to march from

Charles Bell's dramatic rendition of the Zulu attacks on the Trekker encampments at the Bloukrans and Bushmans rivers on the night of 16/17 February 1838. The attacks actually took place during the night, but Bell has captured the surprise, horror and ruthlessness of the assaults. (Wikimedia Commons, public domain)

An incident during the Zulu attacks on the Trekker encampments; a Trekker, Marthinus Oosthuizen, rides through the Zulu lines to deliver ammunition to the beleaguered van Rensburg party on the *koppie* beyond. (uMsunduzi Museum/Author)

eMgungundlovu to the mountain foothills, and they mounted an attack across several miles of difficult country at around midnight on 16 February. During Retief's absence, many of the Trekker groups had drifted from the main concentration in search of fresh grazing, and because many of the men were away with Retief, they consisted largely of women, children, the elderly and Khoekhoe servants, all of whom were unprepared to defend themselves. The Zulu right and centre fell heavily on the families camped along the Bloukrans River, while the Zulu left pushed further south to the encampments on the Bushmans River. Many families were entirely wiped out before the sound of the commotion reached those further back, who were thereby given a brief amount of time to prepare themselves. Along the Bloukrans, in particular, several families gathered in circles of wagons, known as *laagers*, and were not only able to withstand the Zulu attacks, but to send out parties of mounted men to harass the *amabutho* when they retreated. Nevertheless, in a night of bloodshed that would be remembered bitterly into modern times, the Trekkers lost 40 men, 56 women and 185 children, together with as many as 250 of their servants. Thousands of head of cattle and sheep were driven away by the Zulus, leaving the Trekkers not only impoverished but short of food and unable to move their wagons.

Yet the apparent Zulu success belied the fact that the *amabutho* had suffered heavily from even this chaotic Trekker response – the Zulus lost some 500 men in the attack – and failed to entirely destroy the Trekker parties and the threat they posed. Over the following weeks, news of the attack reached Trekker parties in the Transvaal and brought many of them to the aid of Retief's distraught followers, setting the scene for the costliest conflict in the history of the Great Trek and the first committed war between the Zulu kingdom and European interlopers.

CHRONOLOGY

1652	Verenigde Oost-Indische Compagnie (Dutch East India Company) establishes a base in Table Bay to resupply its ships.
1795	The British seize the Cape from the Dutch as part of the wider conflict of the Revolutionary and Napoleonic Wars in France, but return it in 1802 following the Treaty of Amiens.
1799	The Dutch farms on the expanding Cape frontier clash with the amaXhosa people in the first of nine wars against the Xhosa people.
1806	The British defeat Dutch forces at the Cape at the battle of Blouberg and reoccupy the colony.
1816–20	The emergence of the Zulu kingdom.
1820	A sponsored immigration scheme settles 4,000 British settlers on the Cape Frontier.
1824	An unofficial British settlement is established at Port Natal.
1834	Slavery abolished within British colonial territories.
1834–35	The Sixth Cape Frontier War.
1834	First small exploratory treks beyond the boundaries of the British Cape Colony.
1835	The Great Trek begins.
21 August 1836	First clashes between the Trekkers and the amaNdebele kingdom.
20 October 1836	Battle of Vegkop.
17 January 1837	Trekker attacks on amaNdebele settlements at Mosega.
June 1837	Zulu attack on amaNdebele.
4 November 1837	Trekker expedition against the amaNdebele at eGabeni; withdrawal of amaNdebele kingdom.
5 November 1837	Piet Retief visits King Dingane at eMgungundlovu.
11 November 1837	Trekker parties descend the uKhahlamba passes and settle in the foothills.
January 1838	Retief retrieves Zulu cattle from King Sekonyela.
3 February 1838	Retief returns to eMgungundlovu.

6 February 1838	Retief and his followers killed at eMgungundlovu.
16–17 February 1838	Zulu attacks on the Trekker encampments on the Bloukrans and Bushmans rivers.
March 1838	First raid by the 'Grand Army of Natal' on Zulu settlements.
10 April 1838	Battle of eThaleni.
17 April 1838	Battle of the Thukela.
13–15 August 1838	Battle of Veglaer/emaGabeni.
22 November 1838	Andries Pretorius arrives at Trekker encampments in Natal.
3 December 1838	Establishment of a small British garrison at Port Natal.
16 December 1838	Battle of Blood River/Ncome.
20 December 1838	Pretorius' *kommando* occupies eMgungundlovu.
27 December 1838	Battle of oPathe.
June 1839	Zulu invasion of Swaziland, battle of Lubuye.
September 1839	Prince Mpande and followers cross the Thukela River and settle in Natal.
24 September 1839	Withdrawal of the British garrison at Port Natal.
January 1840	Pretorius' *kommando* and Nongalaza's *impi* invade Zululand.
29 January 1840	Battle of amaQongqo.
10 February 1840	Pretorius recognizes Mpande as King of the Zulu.
14 February 1840	Declaration of the founding of the Trekker Republic of Natalia.
15 (?) March 1840	The assassination of King Dingane.
4 May 1842	British troops reoccupy Port Natal.
23 May 1842	British–Trekker battle at Congella, Bay of Natal; start of the siege of the British camp.
25 June 1842	British reinforcements arrive by sea – relief of the siege.
23 February 1854	The Bloemfontein Convention; Britain acknowledges independence of Orange Free State and Zuid-Afrikaansche Republiek (Transvaal).

OPPOSING COMMANDERS

ZULU

King Dingane himself did not take to the field during military operations, but rather appointed commanders from his most trusted and experienced councillors. Nevertheless, the king was deeply committed to the war, taking a keen interest in its progress, and it was ultimately his decisions that shaped Zulu strategy. Dingane had certainly served his time as a young warrior, and he had seen first-hand his brother King Shaka's military prowess. Whereas Shaka had been forthright in his diplomacy and embraced military activity, Dingane was more cautious. He often discussed his true intentions only with his most trusted councillors, and preferred to resort to military action only when he thought his chances of success were overwhelming. In many ways his actions of February 1838 typified his approach; having studied the behaviour of the Trekker leader Piet Retief, and deciding him a danger to the Zulu kingdom, Dingane had used treachery as a means of neutralizing Retief and his immediate followers, and acted to quickly remove the entire Boer threat in a way which, he hoped, would pose the minimum risk to the Zulu army and to

A group of young warriors in the ceremonial uniform of their *ibutho* at the time of the Anglo-Zulu War. Each *ibutho* wore dense coverings of cow tails over the body, and a distinctive and uniform headdress of feathers fixed in a stuffed headband of wild cat or otter skin. In this case, the regiment is wearing a type of headdress known as *amapovela*, consisting of stiff 'horns' of white cowhide with cow tails attached to the tips, and a tall plume of feathers of the *isakabuli*, the long-tailed widow bird. (Author)

the kingdom as a whole. In the fighting that followed King Dingane sought to direct his army to concentrate swiftly and effectively against the various threats that the Trekker and settler forces posed to him, and the army at each phase of the war was usually gathered at eMgungundlovu, ritually prepared, then despatched to fall quickly on its designated target. This was a policy which, of course, left the neutralizing of the very real threats posed by the Trekkers' guns, wagons and horses to the command of his field commanders, and when the initial Zulu successes failed to prevent further attacks, King Dingane became increasingly frustrated with his generals.

The man who fulfilled the role of senior adviser and commander-in-chief of the Zulu army was **Ndlela kaSompisi** of the Ntuli people. A contemporary of King Shaka, and therefore aged around 50 in 1838, Ndlela was connected to the Zulu Royal House through his sister, Bhibhi, who had been King Senzangakhona's (Shaka's father) favourite wife. Ndlela himself had risen to prominence in Shaka's wars and had become a 'companion of the eating mat', a select group of warriors with whom the king would relax and talk over old wars. Ndlela had taken a prominent part during the significant wars between the Zulu and the Ndwandwe kingdom, and had been badly wounded at the battle of Mhlatuze in 1818, but had survived – according to one account he had been dragged out from under a pile of enemy dead after the battle having been stabbed several times. A tall man turning to fat in middle age, he was an experienced commander and had led King Dingane's army in recent years, on an unsuccessful campaign against the Swazi in 1836 and much more triumphantly against the amaNdebele kingdom across the uKhahlamba mountains in 1837. He was considered a thoughtful and measured general but, whilst he had seen the effects of small groups of Port Natal musketmen fighting in Zulu service he had, like all other Zulu officers, not commanded Zulu troops in action against significant numbers of men with guns. Throughout the war of 1838–40 his actions showed that, when not constrained by King Dingane's sense of urgency, he understood his enemy's strengths, and was prepared to develop tactics to overcome them. In particular on several occasions he deployed ambushes very effectively.

Ndlela's second-in-command was another of King Dingane's senior advisers, **Nzobo kaSobadli** – who was widely known as Dambuza – a portly, bad-tempered man with, it would turn out, an unswerving loyalty to the king and a haughty disdain for the kingdom's enemies, which frequently led him to advocate uncompromising strategies. Like Ndlela, he had taken part in various early campaigns, and in peacetime he controlled a section of the huts occupied by assembled warriors at eMgungundlovu with a famously firm hand.

Although Ndlela and Nzobo led the main Zulu armies despatched from eMgungundlovu, other commanders were appointed to armies operating elsewhere in the country, particularly those in the south-eastern districts, close to the Thukela River. Among these was **Prince Mpande kaSenzangakhona**, the King's younger brother. Dingane had ruthlessly purged potential rivals from the Royal House, but had tolerated Prince Mpande because of the latter's lack of obvious ambition and apparent indolence. As a result, Prince Mpande's role in the fighting of 1838 has been largely dismissed and credited to his junior officers, but Mpande was in fact an astute political adviser who was pursuing his own agenda, and it is therefore possible that his military prowess has been similarly underestimated. In the field, Mpande was

Two *izinduna* – officers – energetically debate the merits of an *ibutho* before King Dingane. This ceremony was designed to argue the case for an *ibutho* to be granted the honour of new regimental shields. Across its life, a Zulu regiment would move steadily from carrying predominantly dark shields to predominantly white ones. (Author)

supported by a favourite, **Nongalaza kaNondela**, who had been appointed a commander of the uHlomendlini *ibutho* by King Shaka and served as Mpande's chief *induna* (officer). Also in Mpande's command group was **Zulu kaNogandaya** who, like Ndlela, had been a favourite warrior of King Shaka, and had been wounded in the arm and foot at the battle of Mhlatuze against the Ndwandwe people 20 years before. A thick-set, physically powerful man, Zulu was regarded with considerable awe because of his fierce reputation, and is widely accounted the true commander of Mpande's forces during the early stages of the war.

For all the new challenges which faced them, the Zulu commanders in 1838 were, for the most part, highly experienced men who understood well the strengths and weaknesses of the men under their command.

VOORTREKKER

The murder of Piet Retief at the start of the Trekker–Zulu conflict had deprived the Voortrekkers of their obvious leader in Natal, and his military capabilities remained untested. In the dark days after the attacks on the Bloukrans and Bushmans encampments, the Trekkers looked instead to the leadership of two other parties, both of whom had previously been reluctant to wholeheartedly ally themselves to Retief's plans: Petrus Lafras Uys and Andries Hendrik Potgieter.

Petrus Lafras 'Piet' Uys was a member of a prominent Cape Frontier family, and he had brought not only his extended family but many of his friends on the Trek. Born in 1797, he had first served on *kommando* in the Fifth Eastern Cape Frontier War of 1819–20, and had recently been heavily involved in the Sixth (1834–35) where he had risen from being a field cornet

Andries Pretorius, the confident and meticulous Trek leader who joined the beleaguered Trekker encampments in Natal and was responsible for reviving their military fortunes. This portrait shows him recovering from the injury he suffered at Blood River. (Author)

to being a commandant, and his bravery had been officially noted. A thick-set man with a tangled beard, Uys was noted for his deep religious faith and for his temper, but he was a popular man who had only gradually turned his back on British authority and set his mind on trekking. Uys' family had suffered heavy financial losses in the last Frontier War, and Uys was particularly irritated by the shortcomings in the British compensation system following the emancipation of the Cape's slaves. He had led one of the first tentative expeditions to scout out the possibility of an exodus from the Cape, and already had some knowledge of Natal's political and geographical landscape. **Andries Hendrik Potgieter** was born in the Eastern Cape in 1792 and was something of a contrast to Uys; tall and charismatic, he was a member of the Dopper sect of the Lutheran church, and habitually wore the straw hat and short jacket that they preferred to demonstrate their allegiance. Potgieter was also a veteran of the Fourth and Fifth Frontier Wars, and deeply disillusioned with British rule.

Both Potgieter and Uys had been heavily involved in the Trekker war against the Ndebele in 1836. The war had begun when some Trekker parties had trespassed unwittingly into Ndebele territory and had been attacked. It was Potgieter who had been the principal Trekker commander when the Ndebele attacked the *laager* at Vegkop on 20 October 1836, and Potgieter had triumphed using the tactics that were rapidly becoming the Trekker norm in such conflicts. Potgieter had ridden out with a small number of men and goaded the Ndebele into the attack, falling back before them and taking refuge in the *laager*, allowing the Ndebele to exhaust themselves in unsuccessful attacks on the wagons. Three months later Potgieter had led a successful mounted attack on Ndebele settlements, and in October 1837 Potgieter and Piet Uys had combined together to attack the centre of the Ndebele kingdom at Mosega. In a running fight they had caught the Ndebele by surprise, and attacked a string of settlements in turn, exploiting the mobility of their horses to constantly harass the Ndebele, break up their formations and retire before they could be caught by any counter-attack. By 1838 it was said that Potgieter and Uys were at loggerheads, and found working together difficult. While both were strong-willed and individualistic, these claims may be exaggerated since they managed to put aside their differences when fighting the Zulus. This would prove crucial to the survival of the hard-pressed encampment in Natal since both men were highly experienced in exactly the type of warfare the Zulus chose to wage.

Although not primarily a military commander, **Sarel Celliers** was a leading figure in the Trek. Born in 1801 on the Eastern Cape, Celliers was by the 1830s a short, stocky man with a confident and outgoing personality. Deeply religious, he became for a time the Trek's spiritual guide, encouraging the

Trekker defiance of the Ndebele in 1838, and providing a religious element which helped unite the *kommando* during the Blood River campaign. It was Celliers who led the Trekkers in prayer every evening, and framed the vow which bound them to build a Church to honour any victory God might grant them. During the war, another farmer from the Grahamstown district on the Eastern Cape would emerge as a skilful scout and determined military leader; **Johan Hendrik de Lange**, known as 'Hans Dons', had travelled extensively in the interior before the Trek and was also experienced in warfare on the Cape Frontier.

In the later stages of the war, **Andries Wilhelmus Jacobus Pretorius** emerged as a natural leader among the Trekkers. He was born in 1798 and, like Potgieter, was a native of Graaff-Reinet. Tall, a good orator with a charismatic personality and a confident self-belief in his military skills, Pretorius had joined the Trek late and had arrived in Natal after the Trekker defeats of April 1838. However, his natural leadership, at a time when the Trekkers were dispirited by a string of setbacks, allowed him to emerge as the natural candidate to lead the decisive Trekker campaign of November and December 1838.

So few were the Natal settlers who fought in 1838, and so brief and unsuccessful their part in the war, that none of them emerged as a significant leader. **Alexander Biggar** was perhaps the most significant military influence among them, an Irishman born in 1781 who had served in the British Army as paymaster to the 85th Regiment, but who had resigned due to accounting irregularities and gone to Africa as an 1820 settler. In 1836, he had moved with his family to Natal, where he had tried to organize a volunteer force among the settlers. Biggar's youngest son, George, was killed in the Zulu attacks on the Bloukrans River. Another of Biggar's sons, Robert – who lacked his father's military experience – led the ill-fated Port Natal expedition in April 1838. Alexander Biggar himself led a party of African auxiliaries from Port Natal to join Andries Pretorius' expedition in November.

OPPOSING FORCES

Although very different to one another, both the Zulu and Voortrekker military systems were essentially part-time citizen militia, very different from the conventional systems practised among the major powers of Europe

ZULU

All Zulu men were required to give a period of service to the military. This service began in their late teens, when they were called together from their homes across the country and formed into regiments known as *amabutho* (sing. *ibutho*). The *amabutho* system was central to the evolution of the Zulu state as it was the means by which the most powerful elements in Zulu society – the productivity and military resources of its men – were taken out of the control of the regional chiefdoms who made up the country and placed

LEFT
A young Zulu man carrying a full-sized regimental war shield, *isihlangu*. The duty of serving the king in the *amabutho* fell largely to younger men; marriage was an important rite of passage in Zulu society which marked the onset of adult responsibilities. The Zulu kings assumed the right to allow men to marry, and this was granted only when an *ibutho* was nearing the end of the most active period of its service. The change in status was marked by the adoption of a ring of fibre and gum woven into the hair. (Author)

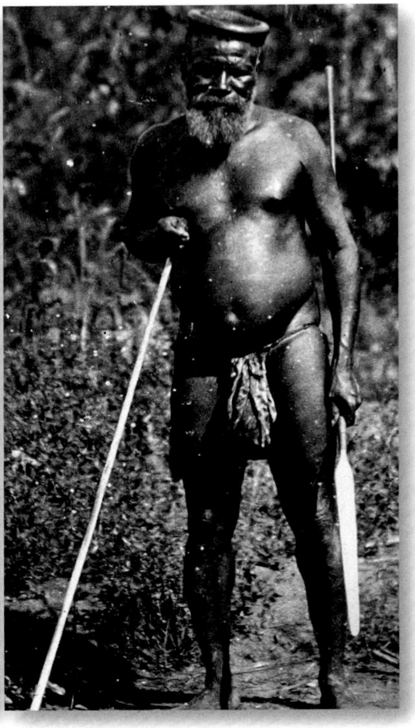

RIGHT
A 19th-century Zulu man wearing the *isicoco*, the head ring, which reflects his status as the head of a family household. He is carrying an impressive example of the characteristic Zulu fighting weapon, the *iklwa* stabbing spear. (Author)

KwaKhangela, a royal homestead in the coastal region of the kingdom. These *amakhanda* served as centres of royal authority and barracks where the men were quartered when they were assembled in the king's service. (Author)

directly in the hands of the king. New *amabutho* were formed every few years, and each *ibutho* therefore consisted of men of the same age, who would remain in the same units throughout life, growing old together. Although *amabutho* were not full-time bodies, as each one was formed it was either directed to build a new royal homestead, which would serve as its barracks when it was assembled on duty, or was incorporated into an existing royal homestead which needed bolstering. Each of these homesteads consisted of concentric rows of domed thatched huts, arranged in a great oval to create a central open space that served both as a pen for the nation's cattle-herds and a parade ground. These homesteads were known as *amakhanda*, 'heads', meaning of royal authority and of the nation. In King Dingane's time, the most favoured royal homestead, where the king spent most of his time, was eMgungundlovu, which was 500 yards across, consisted of upwards of a thousand huts and when fully occupied could accommodate as many as 6,000 men from nine different *amabutho*.

When an *ibutho* was newly formed, it was given a distinctive name by the king and organized into two wings, each of which was further divided into companies, known as *amaviyo*. The size of an *ibutho* was not standard – it depended upon the population demographic in the year in which it was formed – but in King Dingane's time, most *amabutho* averaged between 800 and 900 men. A senior commander – in effect the regiment's colonel – was appointed by the king and his council from older men who had acknowledged experience as military commanders. Each wing of the regiment also had its own subordinate commander, while officers for the *amaviyo* were selected from among young men within the companies who had shown initiative and daring. A newly formed *ibutho* would be quartered at its appointed homestead for several months while the young men grew used to their position, to their appointed officers and to a degree of basic training, much of which consisted of marching and manoeuvring in formation. During that time, the men were fed from a ration of cattle provided by the king, whilst

An engraving showing three orders of dress of a Zulu man during the heyday of the kingdom. On the left, a man wears his everyday costume, while in the centre, a warrior in a young *ibutho* wears his full ceremonial costume. On the right is a senior man wearing the typical dress of an older *ibutho*, including a single long crane feather in his headdress. Note the differences in the colouring of the war shields. (Author)

family members were allowed to bring them additional fresh produce. Life in the *amakhanda* was far from comfortable, however, as the food ration was seldom adequate, young men slept four or five to a room and there was a boisterous, aggressive atmosphere that sometimes erupted into stick-fights when two *amabutho* were too closely quartered together. The strength of personality necessary to control this atmosphere was an essential qualification of the senior officers, who did not baulk at using sticks to enforce their authority if their men became unruly.

For these reasons, however, *amabutho* were not usually kept assembled in their barracks for long periods. After their initial period of training, a newly formed *ibutho* was allowed to stand down, the men returning to live among their families in their ordinary homesteads. They were, however, subject to

Photographs of two pairs of surviving examples of full-sized *isihlangu* regimental war shields, dating to the end of the independent kingdom and the British invasion of 1879. Note how the natural patterns of the hide were utilized to present a regimental uniformity; the darker pattern is from a younger regiment and the white shields (with red spots) from a senior one. (Author)

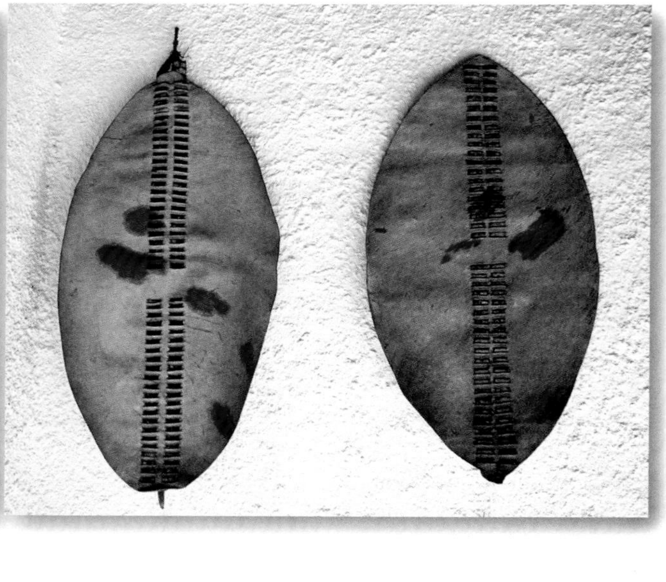

King Dingane reviewing an *ibutho*, a Zulu regiment, on its return from a campaign. (Author)

a call-up whenever their services were required. The king would send the order to his representatives in the outlying districts, and from there the call was passed by shouting from hilltop to hilltop. The men would make their way firstly to the nearest royal homestead, to meet their fellows who lived locally, and then to their own barracks. Despite the distances involved, an *ibutho* could usually be assembled in a matter of days.

Although the *amabutho* certainly comprised the Zulu army, their duties were not confined to the military. They also provided the state labour gang, were frequently used to herd the nation's cattle stock and might be used to repair a royal homestead, or to plough any cultivated fields associated with it. They also took part in large-scale hunts organized by the king, and the participation of the entire army was required for important national ceremonies, such as that which initiated and blessed the annual harvest.

When an *ibutho* was first formed, the king appointed them a herd of cattle from the national herd, which were carefully matched according to the colour of the hide. Sufficient of these cattle would be slaughtered to provide war shields for the men, which therefore had a uniform appearance within an *ibutho*. The selection of these colours reflected a colour-coding system, which demonstrated the age and experience of the men; a new *ibutho* was traditionally granted black or brown shields, but these would need to be replaced every few years and the issue of new shields was a matter of considerable ceremony. The *ibutho*'s commanders were required to demonstrate the worthiness of their men, often in the face of challenges posed by the king's councillors. When an *ibutho* was finally judged worthy, new shields of a different pattern

A Zulu man dresses his friend's *isicoco*, the circle of fibre and gum which marked the estate of a married man. (Author)

Zulu warriors in full regalia. Each *ibutho* had its own particular combination of costume, headdress and shield colour. Although by the Anglo-Zulu War of 1879 the wearing of these costumes on campaign had fallen into disfavour, they were still retained in action by King Dingane's *amabutho*. (Author)

would be issued. A young regiment moved from black shields to black with white patches, each subsequent issue bearing more white until an *ibutho* that had been in service for 20 years or so might carry an all-white shield. These shields, called *isihlangu*, were large enough to cover a man from chin to knees and strong enough to deflect thrown spears or a vigorous stab.

They were not the property of the individual, but rather of the state – they were kept in special storage huts raised off the ground, away from the damp and rodents, in the *amakhanda*. They were issued when an *ibutho* assembled, being returned again when they dispersed after their duties.

Although Zulu men remained enrolled in their *ibutho* throughout life, their service was limited by the onset of family obligations. Until a Zulu man married, he was considered a junior part of his father's homestead, and as such it was his duty to serve his father in menial tasks and, by extension, the higher authority of the king. When he married, however, taking a wife or wives, he left his father's homestead and built his own, starting his own family. Only at that point was he considered an adult with his own responsibilities. Marriage was, therefore, a hugely important rite of passage within Zulu society, marking the point at which a man was no longer immediately responsible for duty in the king's *amabutho*. As a result, successive Zulu kings took to themselves the right to grant permission for men to marry, and this was usually only granted to an entire *ibutho* who had accomplished something like 20 years' service. The decision to allow an *ibutho* to marry was usually announced at the annual harvest festival, and was eagerly awaited by *amabutho* whose members were now in their late 30s or early 40s. Once the decision was announced, the chosen *ibutho* was allowed to disperse and the men would marry their girlfriends in ordinary civilian ceremonies. Thereafter, although they were still subject to service in times of national emergency, they passed into the equivalent of a reserve as the regular duties of serving the king fell to those *amabutho* younger than themselves who were still unmarried.

The change in status was so significant that it was marked by a physical change in appearance – married men adopted a ring of fibre, plastered with gum and beeswax and known as the *isicoco*, on the crown of their heads.

In addition to a uniformly pattered shield, the *amabutho* wore a complex ceremonial dress with headdresses that varied from regiment to regiment. The basis of the headdress was a stuffed headband of wild cat – for younger regiments – or otter skin, and long flaps of monkey skin hung over the cheeks and shoulders. Bunches of specific feathers, as directed by the king, were worn at the back or front of the head, whilst the long glossy tail feathers of the *isakabuli* (widow bird) were worn on either side of the head. Senior men wore long crane feathers at the front of the headdress, and men of royal blood wore small bunches of the red and green feathers of the purple-crested lourie. Dense masses of the fluffy ends of cow tails were worn from a thick necklace so as to hang to the waist at the front and knees at the back, and tails were also worn attached to thongs above the elbow and below the knee. Loin coverings consisted of a thin leather belt with a mop of twisted skins hanging at the front and a square of soft calf's hide over the buttocks. On ceremonial occasions, individuals were almost entirely concealed by this costume. In later years – particularly during the Anglo-Zulu War of 1879 – the habit of wearing these costumes in action was largely abandoned. However, in both King Shaka and King Dingane's day, it was still common to wear much of it in action, although it is possible that the cow tail body ornaments were sometimes replaced with a lighter and less cumbersome equivalent.

A Zulu *inkosi* (chief), Ngoza kaLudaba, wearing his ceremonial dress, the typical finery of a man of rank. He wears overlapping tails made from soft, twisted skins over his body, and a single crane feather on his head. (Author)

During the rapid expansion of the kingdom in King Shaka's time, the army had consisted of a large number of *amabutho*; however, as part of the conciliation of his power following the coup of 1828, King Dingane had merged several of King Shaka's old *amabutho*, bringing them more tightly under his control and giving them new names. Although older *amabutho* still existed, Dingane preferred to deploy a smaller number of younger regiments which were more directly under his control, both at eMgungundlovu, and at royal homesteads in the outlying areas controlled by his most trusted subordinates. It is estimated that in 1838 he had a total of some 20,000 warriors at his disposal.

Although shields were the property of the state, individual warriors were expected to supply their own offensive weapons. Principal among these was a long-bladed, short-hafted stabbing spear, the *iklwa*, which had been a crucial part of the military ideology of King Shaka's day. Warriors were taught to use it in combination with the shield, striking upwards with the shield to catch an opponent off-guard and block his movements and then delivering an under-arm stab at his exposed chest or stomach. As youths, in the years before their military service, young Zulu men were adept at wielding weapons and sticks for everyday protection in the bush, as well as when sparring with one another, and under training they became equally efficient at using the stabbing spear and war shield. In civilian life, the use of light throwing spears was common, but King Shaka, who advocated hand-to-hand combat as a warrior ideal, barred them from use in warfare. However, King Dingane allowed his men to carry them in addition to their stabbing spears – two or three were carried behind the shield, and were thrown at the enemy at a range of 20 or 30 yards as the Zulus charged to attack. The decision to reintroduce them may have reflected an awareness of the longer-range weapons and mobility of new enemies like the Voortrekkers.

As well as the physical paraphernalia of warfare, the Zulu army placed great importance on spiritual reparation. An army was called together several days before embarking on a campaign to undergo ceremonies designed to bind the warriors together, to cleanse them of any spiritual impurities and to protect them against harm or misfortune. Once they had undergone these ceremonies, the warriors were in a heightened emotional state, focused on battle, and would need to complete further cleansing ceremonies at the end

A pair of photographs dating to the coronation of King Cetshwayo in 1873 depicting the front and back views of a warrior in full regalia. By 1879, this costume was no longer worn in action, but similar costumes were the norm during the war of 1838–40. (Author)

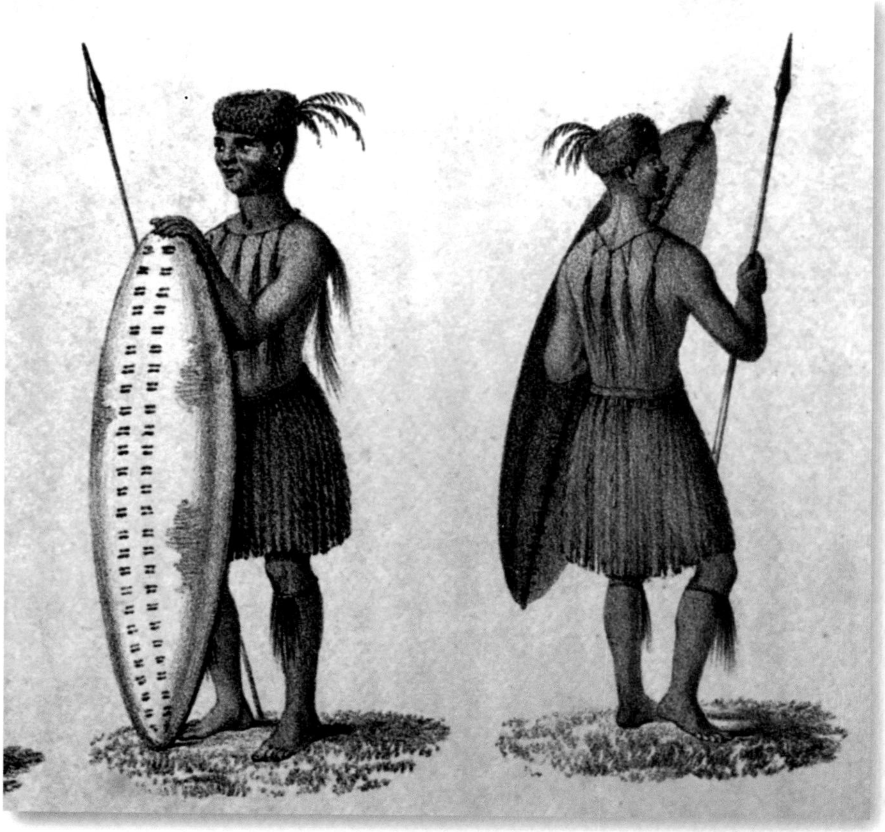

A sketch by Captain Allen Gardiner of Zulu warriors in King Dingane's army. (Author)

of a campaign before they could return to ordinary life. Once launched on campaign, the army would march in two columns, screened by scouts thrown out in advance, with its provisions – a limited supply of live cattle – safely in the rear. Youths not yet old enough to be enrolled in the *amabutho* would carry sleeping mats, headrests and, on longer marches, rolled-up shields for their fathers or elder brothers. Food supplies were usually only sufficient to see the army beyond the kingdom's borders, after which the *amabutho* were expected to live by foraging. Although the distances covered by a Zulu army in a day's march have been the subject of much mythology, a Zulu force could cover distances of 15–20 miles in a day with relative ease, moving through a natural landscape that often confounded European opponents.

The preferred Zulu time of attack was just before dawn, a time known as 'the horns of the morning', when the horns of cattle could first be seen against the lightening sky. Whilst this was intended to catch an enemy off-guard, it also allowed for Zulu commanders to coordinate attacks more easily as they developed in the rising dawn. Because of their dependence upon close-quarter fighting techniques, the Zulus relied upon a battlefield tactic known as the *impondo zankomo* – the horns of the beast – which was inspired by the image of a charging bull or buffalo. While one tactical body – the *isifuba*, or chest – advanced straight at the enemy, flanking parties, composed of younger, more agile *amabutho* – known as the *izimpondo*, or horns – rushed out on either side to outflank the enemy and pin them in

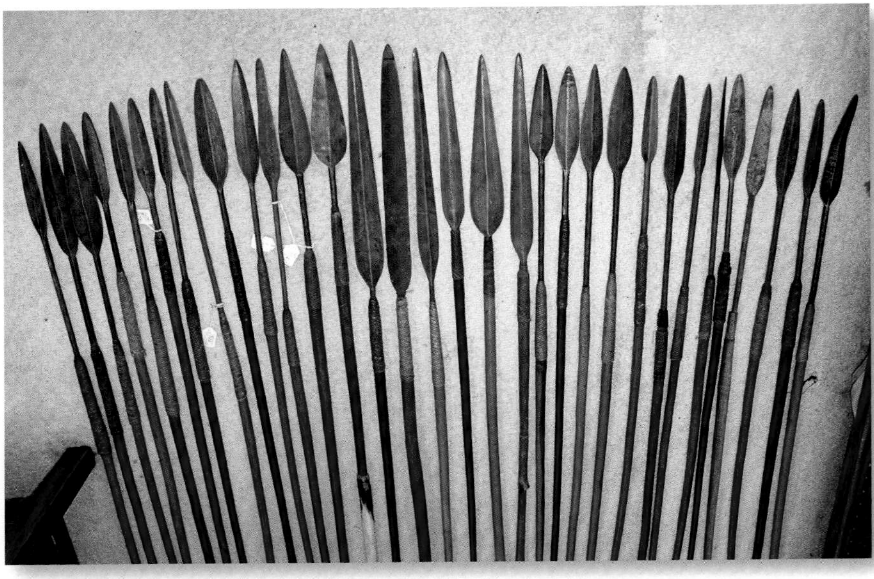

An impressive array of traditional Zulu weapons. The long-bladed examples in the centre are stabbing spears, the smaller-bladed examples on either side throwing ones. (Author)

place. A reserve – the *umuva*, or loins – was kept back to plug attacks as they developed.

The *impondo zankomo* had proved consistently effective against African enemies, but the arrival of the Voortrekkers would require it to be tested in very different circumstances.

In one respect, King Dingane's army included an element that was a new innovation for Zulu warfare: with the death of Piet Retief and his followers, the Zulus captured some 200 horses and perhaps 100 muskets, and more were captured during the attacks on the Voortrekker encampments. From these, the king formed a small mounted unit, the iziThunyisa; although not trained in the use of either horses or guns, they do seem to have functioned to a level of basic efficiency and afforded the opportunity for the Zulus to respond to long-range Boer musketry. Their numbers remained small, however, and they made little obvious impact on the outcome of any of the coming battles.

VOORTREKKER

The Voortrekkers were essentially armed civilians who came together briefly to pursue common military objectives, but who remained farmers and not members of any coherent military organization.

The essence of the Trekker military outlook had been forged on the frontiers of the old Cape Colony, where scattered farming communities in remote areas could seldom rely on regular military forces – whether Dutch or British – to defend them, and who therefore learned to be self-reliant and to band together when necessary with their neighbours. With limited resources to protect their Cape possessions, the Dutch East India Company had required all free burghers between the ages of 16 and 60 to assemble for local defence when called upon to do so, and this system, known as the *kommando* system, was largely inherited by the British. A burgher on *kommando* was expected to provide his own horse, weapons and food, and the system bred a distinct military outlook. *Kommandos* were raised from administrative areas on the frontier, and were usually small – sometimes no more than a few dozen men, and even the largest seldom numbered more than 200–300 – and since men on active service left their families unprotected, often on remote farms, they could not be mobilized for long. With no imposed military structure or discipline, burghers elected their own officers – a *Kommandant* in charge and *veldkornets* in support – and their choices often reflected local social hierarchies or family patronage. Since a *kommando* always remained fundamentally a collection of armed civilians working together in a common cause, a *Kommandant* had no powers to exert control, usually leading by the force of his character or personality; burghers not wishing to obey his directions were at liberty to do so or, in extreme circumstances, simply opt out and go home. While the strength of the *kommando* system was its flexibility and common goals, it also encouraged a parochial outlook, with Boers focused on their immediate needs, sometimes displaying a reluctance to support wider strategic aims or to work in concert with a *kommando* from a different district. Since by definition a *kommando* was composed of individualistic farmers long used to surviving on their own resources in an unforgiving landscape, there was a complete lack of a sense of military honour or glory. The average Boer regarded an armed expedition as a means to achieving a particular end without the undue risk to himself which might leave his family unsupported at home. Furthermore, disputes between individuals and between *Kommandants* were not unusual as opinions were often varied and strongly held, and even the Great Trek was characterized by arguments and feuds between the leaders of different parties, which often hampered co-operation between them.

Since the *kommandos* were not formal military units, the burghers wore no uniforms, but instead attended wearing their everyday clothes. At the time of the Great Trek, check shirts were popular, usually worn with a waistcoat – decorated with embroidery for the fashion-conscious, but sometimes made

A mid-20th century representation of a Trekker *kommando* in the field. Although this sketch is infused with a sense of nostalgia, it does capture the Trekkers' complete lack of military affectation. (Author)

A display of Trekker firearms, a mixture of both flintlock and percussion weapons, some of which are of very heavy calibre. In the centre are powder horns, which the Trekkers generally preferred to wear attached to their waist belts. (Author)

of raw hide, perhaps with the hair left on – or a short waist-length jacket. Trousers were usually of moleskin, and footwear the ubiquitous *veldskoen*, home-made leather shoes. Some men wore neck-cloths tied with a flourish, and the most common headwear was the straw hat, sometimes worn with a cockade of ostrich feathers, although a few more status-conscious individuals wore low top hats.

Weapons, too, were individually purchased. The requirements of frontier life meant that most Boers who joined the Trek were used to shooting in the field for food; this had made them careful not to waste ammunition and a good judge of distance and of a moving target, although the limited capability of most weapons at the time meant few were effective at long ranges. In shooting contests between farmers, a marksman was a man who could hit the knucklebone of an ox at 80 paces. Perhaps the most common type of firearm on the frontier was a smoothbore flintlock muzzle-loading musket similar to the 'Brown Bess' in use by the British Army at the beginning of the 19th century. The more efficient percussion musket had reached the Cape perhaps ten years before the Trek, and was appreciated by hunters who found it quicker to load and less prone to misfires than the flintlock. Some Trekkers were concerned that percussion caps might not be readily available

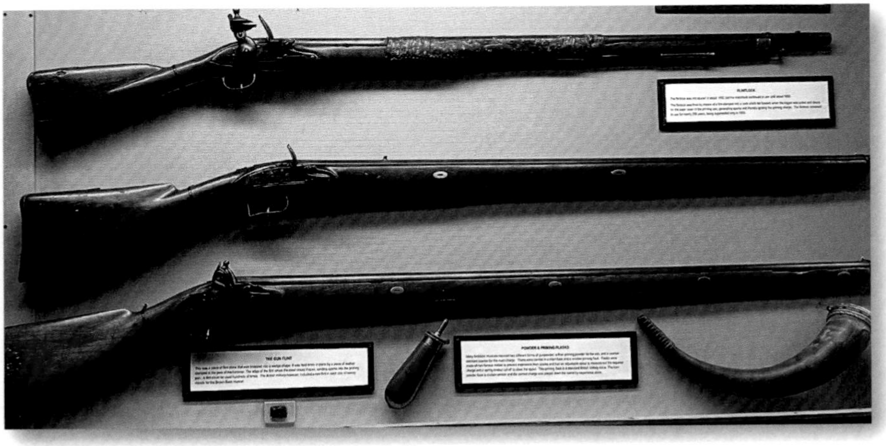

Both the traditional flintlock and the newer percussion models of musket were popular among the Trekkers; note that the top musket has a length of hide stitched round the barrel to protect the firer's fingers against overheating, a common habit among frontiersmen. (South African Military Museum/Author)

The *ossewa* – ox-wagon – was central to the Trekkers' way of life, not only their mobile home but also an effective method of defence. This is a typical *kakebeenwa*, named after the jawbone of an ox because of its distinctive sloping sides at the back. (NJR ZA via Wikimedia Commons, CC BY-SA 3.0)

in the interior and so reverted to the flintlock, but undoubtedly both types were widely used. There were, in addition, a number of locally produced guns that had evolved to suit the frontier market, and these varied from the *bobbejaanboud*, or 'baboon's bum', which had an unusually long and distinctively curved stock, to the double-barrelled 'Cape gun', which boasted two smoothbore barrels, one usually loaded with a number of small balls, like a shotgun, and the other loaded with a single ball, and which thereby offered a hunter or *kommando* a quick choice when hard-pressed in the bush. Those burghers who augmented their income by shooting elephants on the fringes of the Cape Colony often carried a heavy-calibre 'elephant gun', which fired a lead ball weighing 4oz. Powder was carried in powder horns worn on a cord often tied to a waist belt, and most frontier farmers were adept at casting their own lead shot. When fighting against an enemy in close formation, the Boers often used *lopers*, a bag of small balls which exploded after leaving the muzzle and served to devastating effect like a giant shotgun. Although most Boers preferred not to fight at close-quarters – not least because it negated the advantage of their firepower and mobility – most carried a long-bladed hunting knife to which they could resort in an emergency.

Although the core of a *kommando* were the Boers themselves, it seldom functioned without the support of Khoekhoe or mixed-race *agterryers*, who saw to the welfare of the horses and led spares, and acted as cooks and servants on campaign. They were often good shots themselves and fought where necessary. Although the *kommandos* were exclusively a male preserve, Boer womenfolk were often involved in skirmishes in frontier warfare, and the Trekkers were family groups. In a defensive role, when attacked, Boer women were expected to take a supporting role, loading muskets for their menfolk.

The two other props of early Boer military success were the horse and the wagon. The Dutch had imported horses to the Cape from their Indonesian colonies in the 18th century. Across the following century, frontier farmers had bred these into a hardy, stocky local breed, the *Boereperd*, which was noted for its resistance to local diseases and its resilience. The ability to move long distances quickly was crucial to *kommando* military successes, but the burghers were never cavalrymen in the European sense, rather mounted infantry who used horses for transport but preferred to fight on foot. Tactically, when acting offensively, members of a *kommando* would seek out a good position in front of the enemy which allowed for the possibility of a quick escape, would ride to within musket range, dismount, fire – sometimes resting their guns on their horses' backs – then mount up and either retire before their enemy could respond or advance to take advantage of an enemy's withdrawal. Since they were often fighting an opponent who enjoyed a numerical superiority, and who depended on close-quarter combat, it was imperative always to maintain a safe distance and never allow the enemy to come to grips with them.

The other element of Boer success was the *ossewa*, the ox-wagon. Ox-wagons were more than a mobile home for the Trekkers; they were also a means of forming a defensive fortification known as a *laager*. The usual *ossewa* of the 1830s was a long, slim wooden vehicle known as a *kakebeenwa*, named after the jawbone of an ox because of the sloping rear end of the sides. Tough, hardy and designed to withstand long journeys, the *kakebeenwa* was held together with wooden pegs and hide thongs rather than nails so that it could be partially disassembled if necessary to drag over rough terrain. The bed was protected by a canvas hood, and the bodywork was often painted green with jaunty red wheels. A fully laden *ossewa*

The entrance to the bay at Port Natal. British settlers had established a ramshackle settlement there in 1824, but by 1838 their desire to free themselves from the constraints of Zulu rule led them to support the Voortrekkers in their war against King Dingane. (Author)

required a span of 18 oxen in pairs to draw it, and difficult rivers and steep hills often required a double team. Most burghers preferred a type of cattle known as the 'Afrikander', which had a pleasing red colour. On a trek, a wagon was driven by a *Voorlooper*, usually an African servant, who controlled the team with a long hide whip. In dangerous country, Boer parties would camp at night in *laager*, a defensive circle formed by running wagons close up behind one another and passing the shaft, or *disselboom*, under the vehicle in front. Ideally, the livestock, the oxen and horses, would be secured inside the *laager*, although on some occasions the sheer number of animals made this impossible and they were abandoned to the enemy. During the Trek, it was common to employ large *laagers* as a defensive feature in a premeditated battle, with the Trekkers sometimes riding out to provoke an enemy before retreating to the wagons, dismounting and fighting from their protection.

Although most warfare between the Trekkers and African enemies saw the Trekkers at a numerical disadvantage, the skilful combination of horses, muskets and wagons undoubtedly gave them a tactical edge which, properly deployed, could render much larger African enemy armies, dependent upon close-range weapons, largely helpless. Throughout the Trek, the tactical contest saw the Trekkers trying to fight according to their strengths – and their enemies trying to find ways to prevent them.

The French traveller and naturalist, Adulphe Delagorgue, who witnessed the latter stages of the Trekker–Zulu War. Delagorgue's costume – a loose hunting shirt and straw hat festooned with ostrich feathers – was typical of the sort of trans-frontiersmen who made up the settlement at Port Natal. (Author)

PORT NATAL SETTLERS

Whilst the settlers at Port Natal raised an army in support of the Voortrekker attacks on King Dingane, and were like the Boer frontiersmen, there were significant differences in their military outlook. The settlers were primarily of British descent, and therefore not raised in the *kommando* tradition; instead, several of them had prior experience as members of the British Army and Royal Navy, and this influenced their approach to fighting. The prominent settler, Alexander Biggar, was a former paymaster of the 85th Regiment, and had raised a short-lived volunteer unit among the settlers for the defence of the port. Another settler, Robert Joyce, a deserter from the British Army, used his experience to teach the rudiments of musket drill to the settlers' African followers. The settler forces were small, not even reaching 20 men, although they were supported by 30 of their trained Khoekhoe hunters and as many as 400 African followers armed with smoothbore muskets. As many as 2,500 African followers also joined them, carrying traditional weapons. Unlike the *kommandos*, the settlers did not elect officers – there seems to have been no command structure, and they simply agreed their objectives between themselves.

The settlers were hunters rather than farmers and were armed with a similar array of weapons to the Trekkers, accounts suggesting many of them also carried pistols and naval cutlasses, both of which were easily imported at the port. They were dressed similarly to the Trekkers too, although a loose canvas hunting shirt was also popular, and their years living beyond the reach of European authority and fashion had encouraged a number of exotic flourishes, notably a variety of plumes worn in their battered straw hats. Although most of the settlers possessed horses, their African auxiliaries fought on foot.

ORDERS OF BATTLE

Note: While the forces of the Trekkers and Natal settlers during the various battles are generally well-documented, details of the composition of Zulu forces vary widely, and in some engagements the names of the specific *amabutho* are not recorded at all.

The Battle of eThaleni, 10 April 1838

Voortrekkers

Piet Uys' *kommando* – 150 men
(Of these, Jakobus Uys commanded a rearguard of 40 men)
Hendrik Potgieter's *kommando* – 200 men
(Supported by an unknown number of *agterryers*)

Zulus

Commander: Nzobo kaSobadli
5,000–7,000 men of the umKhulutshane, izinGulutshane and imVokwe *amabutho*

The Battle of the Thukela, 17 April 1838

The Grand Army of Natal

18 settlers led by Robert Biggar and John Cane
30 Khoisan hunters
400 African musketeers commanded by Robert Joyce
2,500 African auxiliaries armed with traditional weapons

Zulus

Overall commander: Prince Mpande kaSenzangakhona
Subordinate commanders: Zulu kaNogandaya, Nongalaza kaNondela, Madlebe kaMgedeza and Butho
5,000–7,000 men drawn from the Hlomendilini emhlope and Hlomendlini mnyama homesteads, among whom the imiHaye *ibutho* was heavily represented

The Battle of Veglaer/emaGabeni, 13–15 August 1838

Voortrekkers

Leaders: Hans Dons de Lange, Johannes du Plessis, Jacobus Potgieter and Joachim Prinsloo Potgieter
150–200 Trekker men, 75 women and children
Unknown number of *agterryers*

Zulus

Commander: Ndlela kaSompisi
100 iziThunyisa (mounted, and armed with muskets)
10,000 men; *amabutho* not specified, but it is noted they were senior men, possibly of the iziMpohlo, uDukuza, amaWombe and uFasimba *amabutho* attached to the eMgungundlovu homestead

The Battle of Blood River/Ncome, 16 December 1838

Voortrekkers

Leaders: Andries Pretorius, with Karel Landman, Hans Dons de Lange, Jacobus Potgieter, Pieter Jacobus, Stephanus Erasmus and Jakobus Uys
464 Boers, approximately 60 wagons and two (or three) ships' cannon
100 *agterryers*
200 wagon-team leaders

Port Natal contingent

Leaders: Alexander Biggar, Edward Parker and Robert Joyce
60 African auxiliaries with muskets

Zulus

Commanders: Ndlela kaSompisi and Nzobo kaSobadli
10,000 men, including 200 iziThunyisa (mounted and armed with muskets)
Left horn: iziThunyisa, uDlambedlu and imVokwe *amabutho*
Right horn: izinGulutshane and umKhulutshane *amabutho*
Chest: iziNyosi and uDlangezwa *amabutho*
Loins: uKhokhothi *ibutho*

The Battle of oPathe, 27 December 1838

Trekkers

Leaders: Karel Landman and Hans Dons de Lange
300 men

Port Natal contingent

Alexander Biggar and 60 auxiliaries armed with muskets

Zulus

5,000 men including the uDlambedlu *ibutho*

The Battle of amaQongqo Hills, 29 January 1839

King Dingane's forces

Commanded by Ndlela kaSompisi
5,000 men
Left horn: uDlambedlu *ibutho*
Right horn: iziNyosi *ibutho*
Chest: umKhulutshane, imVokwe, iziMpholo and uKhokhoti *amabutho*

Prince Mpande's forces

Commanded by Nongalaza kaNondela
5,000 men
Left horn: imiHaye *ibutho*
Right horn: elements of the uMlambongwenya, uDukuza and isiKhlebe *amabutho*
Chest: uZwagendaba *ibutho*

OPPOSING PLANS

King Dingane's initial intention had been to destroy the Voortrekker presence entirely in Natal, and thereby eradicate the threat to the Zulu kingdom. His failure to do so in the attacks on the Trekker encampment in February 1838 was dangerous to his people since it strengthened the Boer resolve, not only to remain in Natal but to punish Dingane and preferably severely weaken the capacity of the Zulu army to pose any future threat to Trekker settlement in the area.

Although the Zulu army returned from those attacks driving thousands of head of captured cattle, it was clear that their mission had largely failed. For all the damage they had inflicted on exposed settlements, they had neither eradicated the Trekkers entirely nor driven them out, and they had suffered significant casualties – as many as 500 killed – in the fighting around defended positions. It would take several weeks for the Zulu army to undergo cleansing ceremonies and rest before embarking on a further campaign, time which gave the Voortrekkers an opportunity to regroup.

Although this photo was taken in the 1930s, it gives a rare impression of how a Zulu *ibutho* might have looked during the heyday of the independent kingdom. The men are wearing spectacular headdresses of *isakabuli* feathers. During the 19th century, regimental war shields were larger even than this. (Author)

The heavy casualties suffered by women and children during the Bushmans and Bloukrans attacks engendered a deep bitterness and yearning for revenge among the surviving Trekkers; rather than discourage them, it deepened their determination to remain in Natal and defeat King Dingane. (Author)

In the immediate aftermath of the Bloukrans and Bushmans river massacres, the surviving Boer parties sent messages to Trekker groups beyond the uKhahlamba mountains asking for help. Despite their desperate need, there was a reluctance to comply because many of those in the interior, having only recently defeated the amaNdebele, were hesitant to embark on a fresh war not of their own making with the far more formidable Zulus. Nevertheless, two Trek leaders, Piet Uys and Hendrik Potgieter – who between them had driven out King Mzilikazi of the amaNdebele from the highveld – brought their followers into Natal, and by the beginning of March 1838, the Trekkers were contemplating an offensive. They were assisted in this by the British settlers at Port Natal who, although they did not share the Boers' immediate aims, nevertheless saw the conflict as an opportunity to free themselves from King Dingane's authority. In March, therefore, both the Trekkers and the Port Natal settlers made minor raids against African settlements loyal to King Dingane in the Thukela River valley. These inflicted little real damage on the Zulus beyond reinforcing the king's determination to renew his offensive and complete the task of driving the Trekkers entirely out of his sphere of influence.

As a result, the stage was set for two significant battles which took place within a week of each other in April 1838.

THE CAMPAIGN

THE BATTLE OF eTHALENI

At the beginning of April, Uys and Potgieter planned a swift strike into Zululand in the direction of eMgungundlovu. They took no wagons with them, and instead planned a mounted operation, relying on their skill and mobility to avoid being trapped and overwhelmed by the potentially much larger Zulu forces. Although there was undoubtedly some tension between the two men over the question of who deserved ultimate command, they had nonetheless successfully worked together before, and it is likely that the stories that they quarrelled have been exaggerated. However, the expedition rode as two separate *kommandos*, with Potgieter leading 200 burghers and Uys 147. Both parties were undoubtedly accompanied by armed *agterryers* leading pack and spare horses, but their numbers were often not recorded.

The *kommandos* set off from the battered Trekker encampments on 6 April, striking north-east and crossing the Mzinyathi River at a spot that would later become known as Rorke's Drift. They passed over the high plateau above the emaKhosini Valley, from where they could see eMgungundlovu itself, about 5 miles away. On the morning of the 10th, they began to descend the steep and narrow valley of the Nzololo River. Their approach had, of course, been spotted by Zulu scouts, and at the bottom of the valley, where the ground was less steep and the stream flowed through a cluster of hills, the Zulus were waiting for them.

King Dingane had despatched between 5,000 and 7,000 young men, mostly from the umKhulutshane and izinGulutshane *amabutho*, supported by smaller detachments of the imVokwe, under the command of Nzobo kaSobadli, to block their progress. The advantages enjoyed by the Trekkers in terms of mobility and firepower were obvious enough, and Nzobo planned to negate these as best he could by a skilled use of the ground. The majority of his forces were placed on two hills either side of the Nzololo, but a third detachment had been concealed further up the valley, towards the Trekkers, and had remained hidden as the Trekkers rode past; it was then effectively positioned in the unsuspecting Boers' rear.

As the *kommandos* descended the valley, Nzobo attempted to lure them into position by driving a herd of cattle ahead of them, between the two hills where his men were placed. Since cattle were always an important objective to the farmers, especially after their losses in the attacks on their

The battle of eThaleni, 10 April 1838

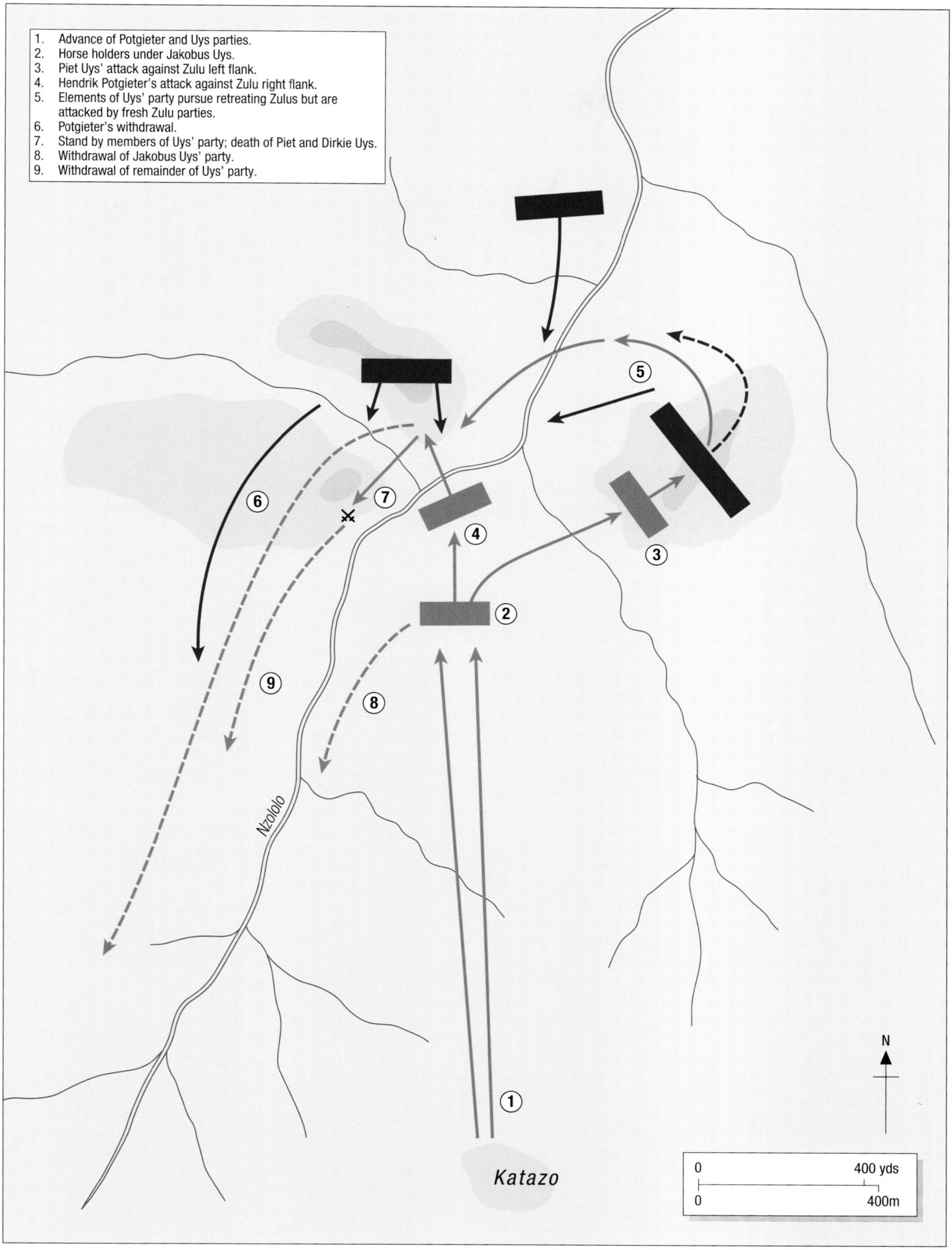

encampments, the *kommandos* obligingly followed them, although both Potgieter and Uys were experienced enough to sense a trap. The expedition's pack horses were left in the rear, guarded by a party of 60 men under Piet Uys' elder brother, Jakobus. The remaining Trekkers then descended with the intention of driving the Zulus off the hills ahead of them, with Potgieter on the left and Uys on the right.

Uys' men began the attack, riding to within 40 yards of the Zulu position before dismounting. Seeing their opportunity, the Zulus rose up and charged, but Uys' men had been ready to fire and loosed a volley at perhaps just 20 yards' range. Few of the Zulus had experienced close-range musketry before, and under the shock and sudden casualties the attack stalled, enabling Uys' men to quickly reload and fire a second volley at almost point-blank range. Stunned, the Zulus began to fall back over the crest of the hill – and at this point Uys' men began to lose cohesion. Encouraged by the sight of the Zulus apparently running, some of Uys' men rode over the crest of the hill and into the valley beyond. The rest refused to follow them, but Uys himself watched as fresh Zulu forces, concealed among mealie fields below, emerged to threaten his over-enthusiastic vanguard. Realizing that they were in danger, he rode forward with 15 men, including his 15-year-old son, Dirkie, to warn them. Once he had separated from those who remained behind on the hilltop, parties of Zulus quickly cut him off, preventing him rejoining them and instead driving the Boers back up along the valley between the two hills, in the direction from which they had come. The Zulus were now making effective use of their throwing spears and showered great clouds of them onto the retreating Boers, several of whom were unhorsed, while Piet Uys himself was hit low in the back by a spear which passed through into his groin.

Dirkie Uys goes to the aid of his stricken father, Piet Uys, during the disastrous battle of eThaleni on 10 April 1838; from a frieze on the Voortrekker Monument in Pretoria. (Joonas Lyytinen via Wikimedia Commons, CC BY 2.5)

Potgieter's party, meanwhile, had been advancing towards the Zulus on the hill on the left when it became obvious that Uys' party was in trouble. In a controversial decision that would lead to bitter wrangling after the battle, Potgieter called off his attack and started to retreat back down the hill. The Zulus on the summit immediately rose up and, rattling their spears against their shields, charged after them, driving the Trekkers off in disarray. The Boer position had now collapsed, with Piet Uys and his rash advance party trying to retire between the hills up the valley of the Nzololo towards Potgieter's men, whilst those he had left on the summit of the right-hand hill – who were standing their ground – were in danger of being cut off. For as much as an hour, those men attempted to hold their position with well-directed musketry, but it was clear that the Trekkers were now in complete disarray. All groups now realized the danger they were in and turned to retreat back up the way they had come that morning. The pack-horse guard under Jakobus Uys attempted to join them, but at that point the Zulu force concealed behind them revealed itself and charged. It proved impossible to lead the pack horses along the rocky and overgrown sides of the valley, and Jakobus Uys was forced to abandon them. The Boers were now in full retreat, with the Zulus in close pursuit. Uys and a handful of men attempted to battle their way up the Nzololo stream, but pressure from the Zulus prevented them from joining with Potgieter's party ahead of them. On the slopes of a stony hill above the stream, Uys – who had pulled out the spear sticking in his body but was exhausted by loss of blood – fell from his horse; realizing he could not be saved, he urged his followers to abandon him, but his son, Dirkie, called out, 'I will die with my father!' and was killed by his side.

The battle then became a running fight as the Trekkers made their way across miles of open country, crossing the Mhlatuze River and passing below the iThala mountain, from which the battle would take its name. Several times, the Zulus manoeuvred quickly enough to almost cut them off, forcing the Boers to dismount and fire volleys to keep them at bay, before mounting up and riding on. The Zulus pursued them for 15 miles before finally giving up.

For the Trekkers, the battle had been a disaster. Although only ten men had been killed, dozens more were wounded, and the *kommandos* had lost a wealth of pack animals and ammunition. The death of Uys and his son, and the disarray and defeat of the two most experienced military commanders in the Voortrekker party, was deeply depressing, and the survivors retreated once again to the doleful camps in the uKhahlamba foothills. There, the incident would become known as the *Vlugkommando* – the *kommando* that ran away.

For the Zulus – whose losses were not recorded, but are likely to have numbered several hundred – the battle was a great encouragement since it proved that Trekker musketry could be negated by skilful generalship. Nonetheless, Nzobo had not quite managed to destroy the *kommandos* entirely, and whilst the threat to eMgungundlovu had been averted, the Boer encampments had not been threatened. Nevertheless, within a week, the combined Trekker/settler position was dealt a further blow by another defeat in the south.

THE BATTLE OF THE THUKELA

At the end of March, the Port Natal settlers had agreed to support the Trekkers in their renewed offensive against King Dingane, and the Trekkers' fresh offensive had afforded the settlers an opportunity to strike in a different part of the country while the Zulus were preoccupied. As important as these strategic concerns, however, was the limited success the settlers had enjoyed in a brief foray across the Thukela a few weeks earlier, which had caught Zulu settlements unprepared and had produced a large haul of captured cattle. A missionary witnessed the settlers' passage on that occasion and gave a vivid impression of them, which reflected their combination of traditional African approaches to campaigning and the exotic blend with European firepower for the coming campaign:

Note: gridlines are shown at intervals of 500m (546.8 yards).

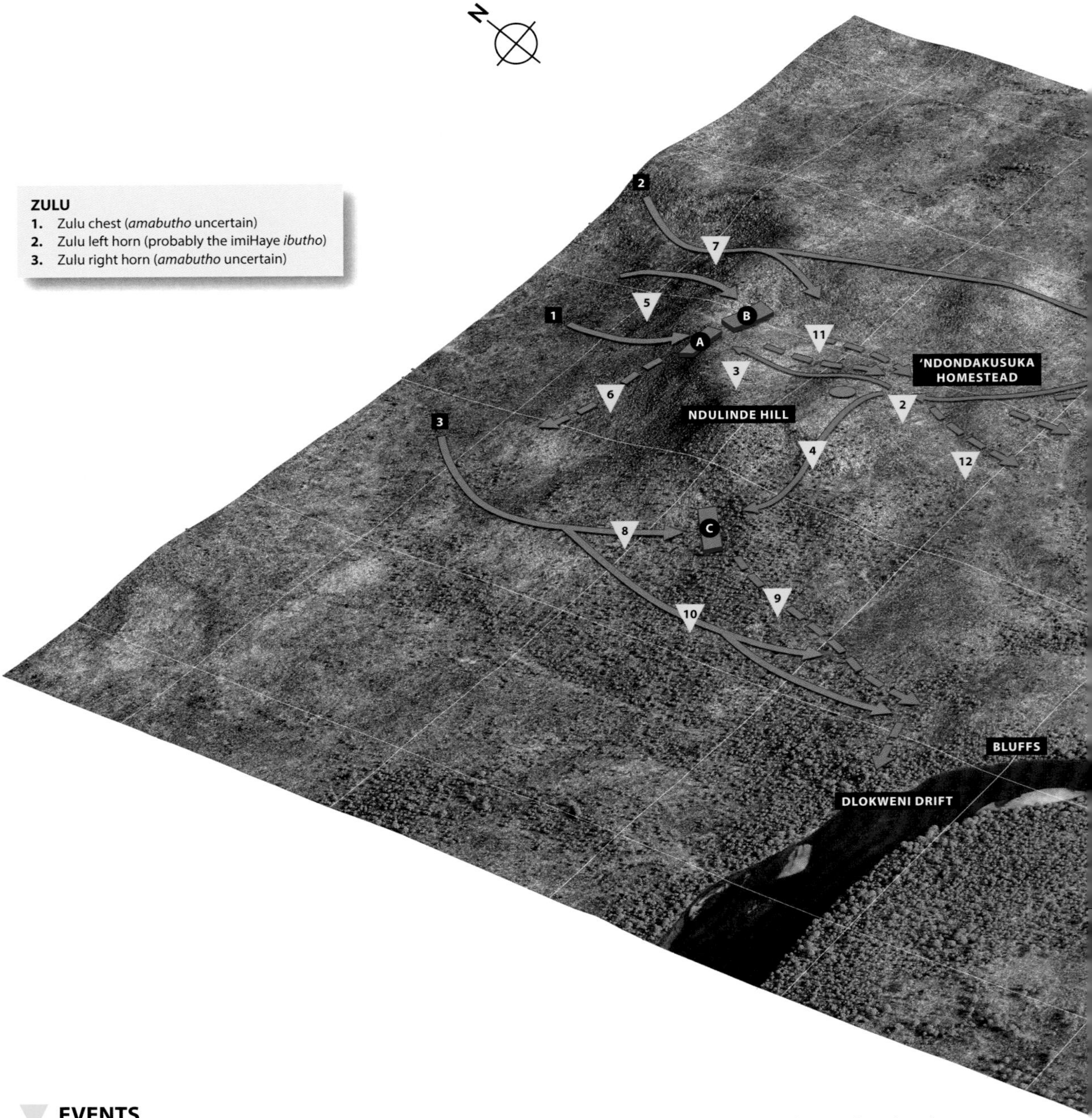

EVENTS

1. The initial advance of the 'Grand Army of Natal' from the Lower Thukela Drift crossing point downstream.

2. The 'Grand Army' deploys before the 'Ndondakusuka homestead which was occupied by the Zulu vanguard; the settler troops fire on the huts and set the homestead ablaze.

3. The 'Grand Army' moves beyond 'Ndondakusuka to deploy against Zulus advancing from beyond Ndulinde hill.

4. Auxiliaries under the command of Henry Ogle move around Ndulinde hill to block any possible deployment by the Zulu right.

5. The Zulu chest attacks the settler forces.

6. The Zulu chest is repulsed and retires.

7. The Zulu left horn makes a fierce attack against the settler right.

8. The Zulu right horn attacks Ogle's detachment.

9. Ogle's detachment breaks under pressure from the Zulu right horn and flees towards the Dlokweni Drift.

10. The Zulu right outflanks Ogle's detachment, driving them away from the drift, trapping them above bluffs overlooking the river.

11. Under pressure from the Zulu left Cane and Biggar's detachments begin to retire towards the river.

12. John Cane is killed.

13. The 'Grand Army' routs back towards the river.

14. The Zulu left horn outflanks the routing 'Grand Army', causing heavy losses on the descent to the river.

THE BATTLE OF THE THUKELA, 17 APRIL 1838, 0600–1000HRS

The view of the battlefield from the south-west, showing the approach of the 'Grand Army of Natal' after crossing the Thukela River, the attack on the homestead of 'Ndondakusuka, the Zulu response and the settler collapse.

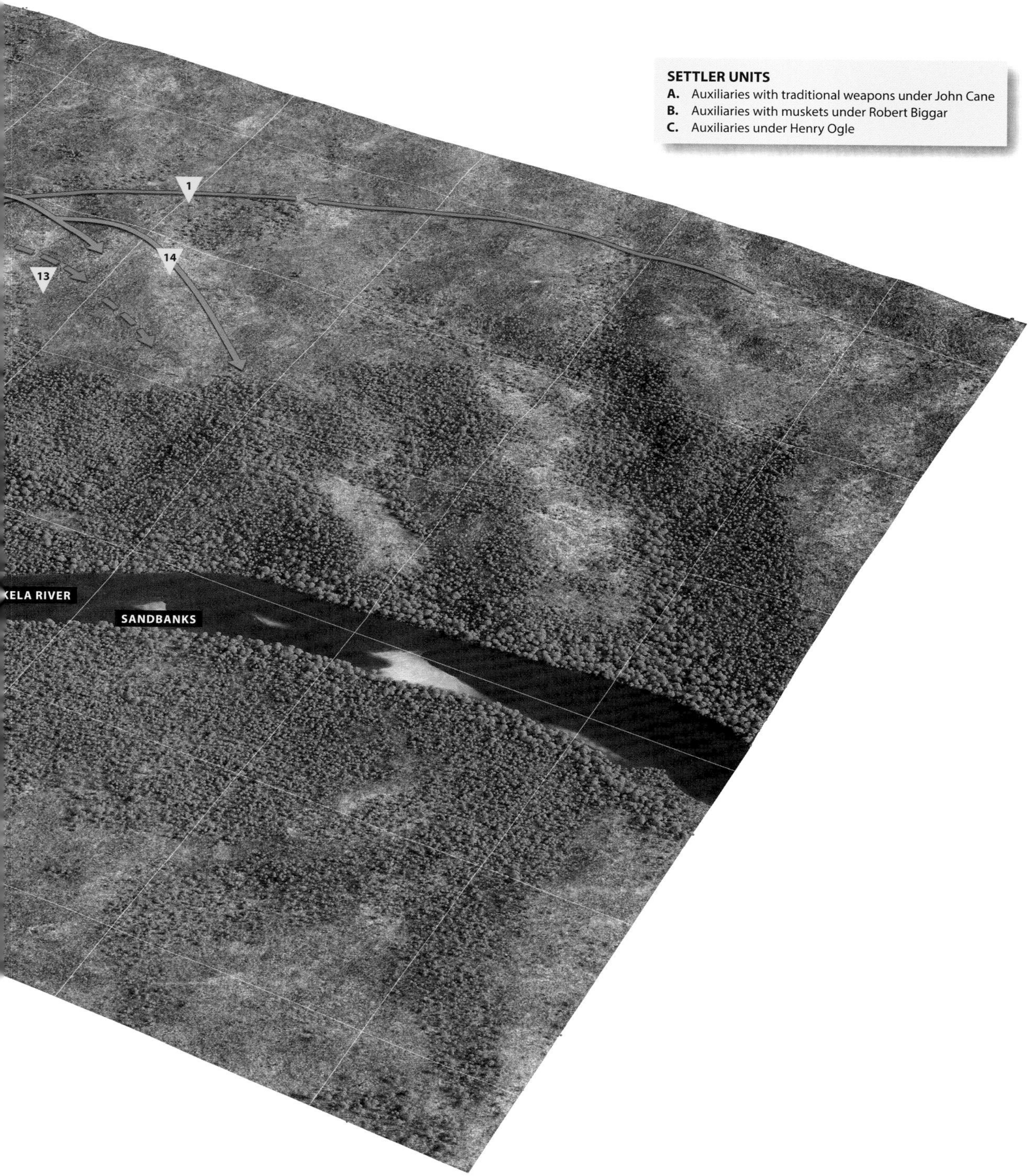

About 400 Zulus [i.e. Natal Africans] came bellowing a war-song. It sounded exactly like the noise of the angry bulls. No one could mistake its angry meaning, its tone was that of angry revenge. The words in English were: 'The wild beast has driven us from our homes, but we will catch him.' They were headed by a white man, who had an old straw hat on, with an ostrich feather stuck in it. He had on his shoulder an elephant gun covered with panther's skin, and walked quite at ease at the head of his party, who went on with their dismal song, except that occasionally they all whistled the Zulu charge. They had flags flying on one of which was written, 'Izin kumbi' (or the locusts), on another 'For justice we fight.' They did not fatigue themselves with jumping or shouting, but the monotonous howl could be heard for two miles. In front they drove cattle for slaughter, in rear the degraded wives carried Indian corn, pumpkins etc, all of which passed so quickly by me that it seemed like a frightful dream.

In mid-April, the settlers decided to make another attempt, this time advancing directly north by the established track that wound up from Port Natal and across the Thukela at the Lower Drift, not far from the river mouth. Although it is unlikely the settlers knew the exact timing of the Uys/Potgieter expedition, they undoubtedly hoped that the Zulus would be distracted, enabling them not only to mount a diversionary attack but also hopefully to carry away a large quantity of lightly protected Zulu cattle.

The settlers assembled a force they rather optimistically entitled the 'Grand Army of Natal'. The leaders were 18 settlers, led by Alexander Biggar's son, Robert, John Cane and John Stubbs, all of them mounted and heavily armed with hunting weapons, pistols and cutlasses. Henry Ogle, an experienced settler who had been involved in expeditions on behalf of both King Shaka and Dingane, did not take part; his followers had quarrelled with the rest of the 'Grand Army' over the division of spoils in the earlier campaign, and he was nursing resentment. Despite pleading sickness, however, he did allow his followers to join the expedition, led by his senior *induna*. The settlers were accompanied by about 30 Khoisan hunters and some 400 African dependants armed and trained in the use of muskets. These men were under the personal direction of Robert Joyce, who had deserted from the 72nd Regiment on the Eastern Cape Frontier and had drifted to Port Natal. Joyce had taught the musket-men the rudiments of British military drill, including volley fire and probably fighting in ranks. A further 2,500 African dependants were assembled, armed with traditional shields and spears; to distinguish them from the Zulus, they were issued with strips of white cloth which they wore twisted around the upper arm. Since the settlers all considered themselves of equal rank, there was no command structure, and their strategy seems to have been decided by agreement among them. Nevertheless, their lack of a clear objective and the simmering differences among the various groups meant that the 'Grand Army of Natal' was dangerously divided.

The 'Grand Army' set out from the Port in two sections, led by Biggar and Cane, and reached the Thukela on 16 April. Scouts reported that the country on the opposite bank appeared largely deserted apart from several herds of apparently unguarded cattle. John Cane apparently suspected that these were a trap, but Robert Biggar argued that the strong force of musketeers would be enough to defeat any Zulu army and, swayed by the prospect of easy plunder, the settlers agreed to cross the river. At dawn on the 17th, they crossed at the Lower Drift – where a column of the British Army would also

The battlefield of the Thukela. The 'Grand Army of Natal' crossed the river at the drift in the foreground before marching on Ndulinde, the highest hill on the horizon in the centre of the photo. The 'Ndondakusuka homestead stood on the slopes towards the right of the hill; the battle raged across country as far back as the drift. In 1838, the terrain was grassland with scattered patches of bush. (Author)

cross during the Anglo-Zulu War 41 years later – and then moved slowly towards a large Zulu homestead known as 'Ndondakusuka on the forward slope of the Ndulinde hill.

As with the Trekker expedition, however, the Zulus had been keeping a careful watch on their progress. Whilst troops from the main royal homestead at eMgungundlovu had been deployed to stop Uys and Potgieter, a force drawn from nearby royal homesteads had been assembled to guard the southern gateway into the kingdom. Numbering some 5,000–7,000 men, these were drawn from a number of *amabutho* quartered in the royal homesteads in the area, but at their core was the imiHaye *ibutho*. The army was commanded by King Dingane's younger brother, Prince Mpande kaSenzangakhona, who lived nearby and knew the country well. The prince was not renowned for his martial skills, but was accompanied by his chief *induna*, Nongalaza kaNondela, who commanded detachments at the nearby Hlomendlini *ikhanda*. To add sound practical experience to the command group, they had Zulu kaNogandaya, who had a reputation as a fierce warrior dating to King Shaka's time, and who lived himself at 'Ndondakusuka. This army had been bivouacking in the hills north of Ndulinde and had moved forward the previous evening in anticipation of the settlers' advance. Whilst most of the army was camped north of the hill, out of sight of the 'Grand Army of Natal', the vanguard had advanced and occupied the huts at 'Ndondakusuka.

The settlers' scouts reported that there were Zulus in the 'Ndondakusuka homestead, but that it appeared to be lightly occupied, and Biggar and Cane directed Joyce's musketeers to advance close to the surrounding palisade and to open a heavy fire into the huts. They kept up this fire for some time, and at one point someone noticed that some of the huts appeared to be sagging from the top, pulled in from the inside. Guessing that this was due to warriors inside trying to avoid the musket balls by clinging to the framework of the thatch, the settler army redirected its fire, and several of the huts collapsed and caved under the fusillade. Jubilant, the 'Grand Army' streamed into

A sketch of the turning point of the battle of the Thukela – the settler army collapses and is driven towards the river. One of the settler commanders, John Cane, is shown on horseback, surrounded by Zulus – he was killed shortly afterwards. (Author)

the homestead, searching for loot and setting fire to the huts. They found a number of dead and dying Zulus, one of whom defiantly urged them to 'Kill me right now, but the elephant is coming and will trample you underfoot!'

The settler attack on the homestead was observed by the Zulu commanders, who had taken up a position on a neighbouring hill and quickly realized that the settler forces were distracted. They urged their troops into battle array and ordered them to advance, the chest sweeping around the shoulder of Ndulinde hill, with the two flanking horns thrown out widely on either side. Feeling was apparently running high among the *amabutho* in indignation at the settlers' betrayal of their former allegiance to Dingane. The advance of the chest, coming around the north-eastern flank of Ndulinde, was soon obvious to the settlers, who regrouped their forces, initially drawing up close to the burning homestead and placing their musketeers in the front and the traditionally armed auxiliaries behind. As the Zulu centre advanced, Joyce directed the musket-men – supported by the fire from the settlers themselves – to open a heavy fire, which soon caused the Zulu centre to halt and retire beyond the slope of the hill.

By this time, the advance of the flanking horns had become apparent, and Cane and Biggar decided to split their forces. While they took the right of the settler line, they directed Henry Ogle's contingent to move to the left of Ndulinde, in anticipation of the attack from the Zulu right. Both sides were now committed to a developing battle which represented a style of fighting not yet seen in Zululand; the settlers were fighting on foot in a manner influenced by British infantry tactics, and very different from the mobile mounted forays of the Voortrekkers, whilst the Zulus had not until this point experienced anything like this intensity of musketry fire. Nevertheless, the Zulus were not in the slightest undaunted by this experience, and their commanders merely sought to use the undulating ground to good advantage to mask them from the worst effects of the musket fire and to try to exploit weaknesses in the lines of the 'Grand Army'. It is difficult to avoid the impression that the experience that Zulu kaNogandaya had earned in his battles fighting for King Shaka stood him in good stead here.

In the event, the battle was decided on the settler left. At first, the Zulu attack had suffered heavy casualties here too, but instead of holding their ground, Ogle's men began to shift to their left, towards the river. They were probably missing the steadying hand of Ogle himself and, perhaps by now feeling increasingly isolated, sought to place themselves nearer to the potential safety of the river crossing. Seeing them slip away, one of the Zulu commanders is said to have called out, 'Oh! They can run, can they?' and urged the Zulus to renew the attack. The right horn pressed forward, some elements sweeping round in an apparent attempt to cut Ogle's men off from the river. Seeing this, Ogle's men suddenly broke and fled, herded away from the nearest crossing point and fleeing instead downstream, with the Zulus among them, stabbing at the slowest. At one point, some of Ogle's men found themselves on a bluff above the river, and with no way down, threw themselves off and into the water rather than be killed by the Zulus behind them.

The collapse of the settler left meant Cane and Biggar's forces were isolated and in danger of being outflanked. Nonetheless, Robert Joyce's musket drill had proved effective, and the 'Grand Army' fire was so devastating that it scythed great gaps in the Zulu lines. Cane and Biggar tried to maintain their formation, retiring slowly passed the burning homestead, hoping to retire to the Lower Drift where they had crossed just a few hours before. By this point, however, the Zulu left had begun to outflank them, threatening to swing round and cut their line of retreat, whilst the flight of Ogle's men on their left potentially left their rear exposed. The fighting was beginning to rage hand-to-hand in places, and the 'Grand Army' was losing the advantage of cohesive firepower. Robert Biggar was surrounded and killed near the

The closing stages of the battle of the Thukela – the 'Grand Army of Natal' is routed and the survivors driven into the river by the victorious Zulus. (Author)

THE CLIMAX OF THE BATTLE OF THE THUKELA, 17 APRIL 1838 (PP.52–53)

The battle of the Thukela represented the first clash between an army influenced by British military techniques and the Zulu army – a scenario which would be played out many times as the century wore on. Although the settlers of the 'Grand Army of Natal' were civilians, one of them, Robert Joyce, was a deserter from the British Army and had trained some of the African auxiliaries in the rudiments of British musketry drill. Although the settlers, in their exotic and individualistic frontier style of dress, had no military structure otherwise, the musket-men were able to check the advance of the Zulus for some time. When the settlers split their command, however – probably due to overconfidence – the Zulu commanders were able to use the ground to shield their men from the worst effects of the settler firepower and outflank the overstretched 'Grand Army' line. This image shows the moment the settler line begins to collapse and retreat past the burning 'Ndondakusuka homestead (**1**). Some of the auxiliaries turned and fled (**2**), many tearing off the white armbands which marked their allegiance, and once the Zulus were able to get close enough to charge, the 'Grand Army' collapsed. Although details of the Zulu force are imprecise, the imiHaye *ibutho* was strongly represented and, as was still common in King Dingane's time, they wore their full ceremonial regalia, which apparently consisted of a bunch of vulture feathers at the back of the head and several tall russet stork feathers at the front (**3**). Their shields were dark brown or black, with white patches on one or both sides (**4**). The use of throwing spears, unpopular in King Shaka's time, proved particularly effective in engagements such as this, a shower of spears offering an opportunity to disrupt the enemy's lines and discourage them from reloading their muskets before a charge hit home (**5**).

homestead. John Cane was riding back with his men when the Zulus caught up with them, and he found himself in a fierce melee and was suddenly struck in both the chest and back by thrown spears. Nestling his musket in the crook of his arm, his pipe still clutched between his teeth, Cane tried to escape but fell from his horse through loss of blood. His last act was to shoot what he thought was a Zulu coming to kill him, but who was, in fact, one of his own men coming to his aid. Another settler, John Stubbs, was stabbed by a young warrior and cried out indignantly, 'Am I to be killed by a boy like you?'

With the death of several of their leaders, the 'Grand Army of Natal' suddenly fell apart, the auxiliaries throwing down their weapons and tearing off their distinctive white armbands before running towards the river. By now, the horns of the Zulu army had almost met, and they pursued the survivors down the length of the river towards the drift, flushing out survivors who tried to hide in the undergrowth. Many of those who did reach the river were drowned as they tried to cross.

Of the 18 settlers who had led the expedition, only four survived – including Robert Joyce – and as many as half their Khoekhoe hunters were killed. So too were perhaps a thousand of their African auxiliaries, whose bones littered the path of the rout for decades to come. Ever since King Shaka had welcomed the Port Natal settlers in 1824, the Zulus had been in awe of their firepower. Now, however, having met them in open battle for the first time, they had decisively routed them, despite suffering heavy losses themselves – as many as 2,000 killed and wounded. Coming so soon on top of the Zulu victory at eThaleni, the battle of the Thukela had effectively shattered the myth of European military invincibility.

The survivors of the expedition trickled back to Port Natal, spreading news of the defeat, and the remaining community there took fright at the thought that the Zulus might follow up their victory. A number took to the bush, whilst others rowed out and took refuge on a boat that happened to be anchored in the bay. Their fears were correct; on 24 April, the Zulus appeared on the outskirts of the settlement and swept through, burning and ransacking the ramshackle huts and buildings, and carrying away everything of value.

Although the settlers would return once the Zulus had gone, the clash had not only ended them as a factor in the war between the Voortrekkers and the Zulus, but had also irrevocably tainted their future relationship with the Zulu Royal House.

THE BATTLE OF VEGLAER

The aftermath of the two Zulu victories produced something of a strategic stalemate. Defeated and dispirited, the surviving settlers at Port Natal, who had hitherto treated the Trekkers as equals, agreed to place themselves under Boer authority in return for protection against further Zulu attacks. This encouraged the Trekkers to consolidate their *laagers* in the uKhahlamba foothills, yet there was no prospect of a peaceful settlement of the region until the war with King Dingane could be resolved, and the failure of the *Vlugkommando* offered no easy solution as to how that might be achieved. King Dingane, on the other hand, while bolstered by his victories, remained cautious that his men might not be able to overcome the Boers in their defensive positions. As the months dragged by, however, both sides hankered for a resolution, and King Dingane was in the best position to act. In August 1838, he reassembled his *amabutho*, had them ritually prepared for war and once again sent them to overrun the Boer encampments. This time they were led by his senior military commander, Ndlela kaSompisi.

The Trekkers had spent the intervening months preparing their camps against such an eventuality, some of the smaller parties combining to form bigger camps which could be more comprehensively defended. At Gatslaer, 290 wagons were lashed in two rows into a triangular-shaped *laager* carefully positioned on a rocky ridge that was protected by a bend in the Bushmans River. The gaps between the wagons were filled with thorn-bushes, while small pits were dug facing the drifts across the river to disrupt any Zulus trying to cross. For the first time, a small ship's cannon was mounted to protect the apex of the triangle. On the morning of 13 August 1838, servants out guarding livestock spotted the approach and the Trekkers hurried into the *laager*. Altogether there were about 70 able-bodied men in the *laager*, together with a large number of women and children.

Ndlela commanded some 10,000 men, many of them more senior *amabutho* quartered at eMgungundlovu, and he deployed them carefully, exploiting the 'chest and horns' formation to fully surround the *laager* out of musket range. Then they began to attack, manoeuvring towards possible weak spots in the Trekker defences. There were not enough men in the *laager* to defend the whole perimeter, and they had to move from one area to another to meet each new attack. Whilst most of the women and children remained in a sheltered enclosure inside the *laager*, a number stayed near the wagons to load muskets for their men. Despite the Zulu determination, the curtain of fire around the *laager* was so destructive that no warriors were able to reach the wagons, and Ndlela called off the attack in the early afternoon. The Zulus were not defeated, however, and spent the night along the banks of the river, slaughtering some of the livestock the Boers had been unable to secure within the *laager*. In the morning, Hans De Lange rode out with a mounted patrol to scout the Zulu intentions, and immediately the Zulu army formed up and returned to the attack. This time, Ndlela ordered his men to try to burn out the defenders, flinging spears tied with straw and set alight into the wagons. Unfortunately for the Zulus, this ingenious tactic failed as the warriors were shot down beyond the reach of their spears, and the wagons remained secure. After a day spent around the *laager*, considering his options, Ndlela once again withdrew to bivouac for the night, but on the third day, before he could renew the attack, a party of 60 Boers from another *laager* arrived to assist the defenders of the Gatslaer. Ndlela opted to withdraw.

The attack on Gatslaer – which the Boers promptly rechristened *Veglaer*, 'Fight Laager', and the Zulus knew as emaGabeni, referring to the 'hunting pits' which the Boers had dug at the river crossing – undoubtedly marked a turning point in the war. The Trekkers had abandoned their usual mobile tactics and instead had worked to perfect the strengths of the *laager* defence, so much so that despite Ndlela's careful and considered response, the Zulus had proved utterly unable to overcome it. The lessons would not be lost on both sides in the decisive campaign to come.

THE BLOOD RIVER/NCOME EXPEDITION

In the aftermath of the unsuccessful attack on the Gatslaer *laager*, a stalemate settled over the Trekker–Zulu campaign. Whilst the Trekkers were encouraged by their undoubted success, they lacked the capacity to follow up their advantage, and it was increasingly obvious to King Dingane that he had few remaining military options to drive out the Boers as he wished. At Port Natal, the surviving British settlers had returned to try to rebuild their settlement, but they were militarily spent.

The impasse was broken in late November 1838 when a new leader, a 40-year-old farmer from Graaff-Reinet in the Eastern Cape named Andries Pretorius, rode into the Boer camps with 60 men and a ship's cannon. Confident and decisive, Pretorius' presence galvanized the Trekkers in their cramped *laagers* and restored a sense of urgency to their cause. Pretorius recognized that if the Trekkers were to remain in Natal, they would have to defeat the Zulu threat once and for all. His determination was strengthened by the news that, in response to the conflict in Natal, the British authorities at the Cape had decided to reassert their claim to Port Natal, and had sent a small military force to occupy it. To Pretorius, the future of any Trekker settlement in Natal depended on prompt assertion of their power and independence. At the end of November, Pretorius issued a summons to the commandants of the various *laagers* in the uKhahlamba foothills, urging them to send men to support him.

Pretorius' expedition was intended as a fighting *kommando*, and was conceived to take advantage of the success at Veglaer and to maximize the Trekkers' strengths in the field. No women and children accompanied it, but Pretorius assembled a large number of wagons which he intended to use as a mobile *laager*, encircling them each night on the march, and then using them to form a fortification upon which he hoped to lure the Zulu attack. The exact number of wagons is, like much of the story of the subsequent campaign, heavily mythologized and subject to heated debate; although the generally accepted figure is 64 wagons, contemporary accounts suggest that there were no more than 60. Although the wagons were loaded only with supplies, powder and ammunition, they still required at least ten oxen each to draw them, and as each burgher rode a horse and led a spare, the expedition was accompanied by as many as 750 horses. A total of 464 Trekkers responded to Pretorius' call to arms, with Pretorius himself in command, Karel Landman as his deputy and five further commandants to share the duties. The expedition was accompanied by a Calvinist pastor, Sarel Celliers, who, to bind the sense of unity, led the *kommando* in

Sarel Celliers, the Calvinist minister who accompanied Pretorius' *kommando* and with him was responsible for drafting the vow, the religious commitment to achieve victory over the Zulus, which helped reinforce the Trekkers' resolve during the campaign. (Author)

The war, May 1838–February 1840

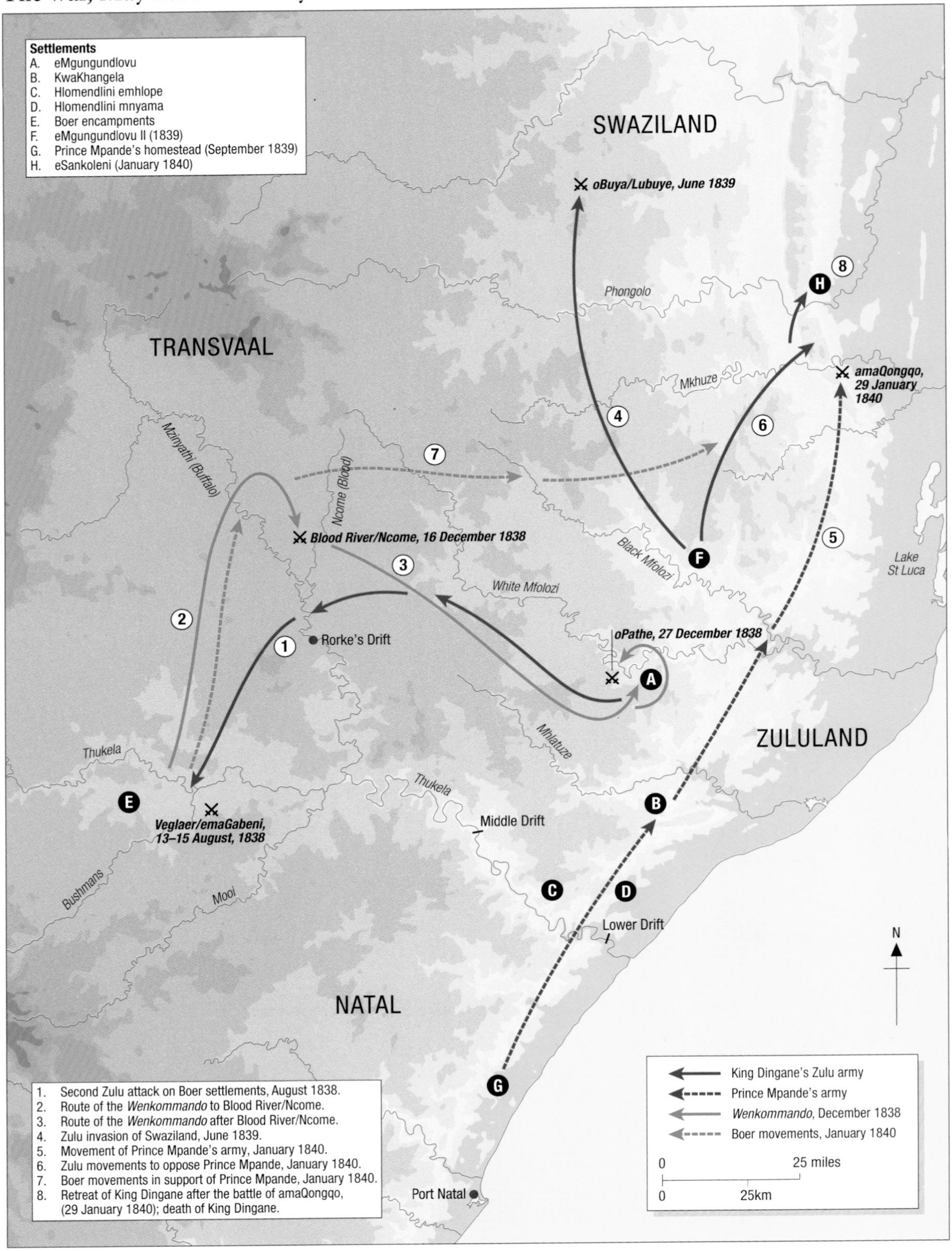

A Zulu *ibutho* crossing a river on the march, the warriors taking the opportunity to drink. The *amabutho* were at home in their environment and could cover terrain which often confounded European enemies. (Author)

prayers each evening and, together with Pretorius, drafted a vow, a covenant with God, in which the Trekkers agreed to hold the day holy should they be granted a decisive victory. In addition to the Trekkers themselves, the Port Natal settler, Alexander Biggar – who was bitter at the death of his sons, George and Robert, at Zulu hands – joined the expedition, together with Robert Joyce, the survivor of the battle of the Thukela, and another settler,

The banks of the Ncome River, where Pretorius established his *laager* on the evening of 15 December 1838. The river flowed sluggishly through a wide floodplain, with thick patches of reeds in places along the banks. According to the Boers, so many Zulus were killed in the river that it turned red with blood. (Author)

The modern monument on the Blood River/Ncome battlefield consists of 64 bronze wagons standing – more or less – on the spot they occupied during the battle, with the distinctive shape of Vegkop behind. The centre of the *laager* is deceptively empty; during the battle it was full of hundreds of trek oxen and horses. (Author)

Edward Parker, who between them brought about 60 African auxiliaries armed with muskets. Managing oxen and horses required the presence of around 130 wagon drivers and team leaders, along with 100 *agterryers*. Pretorius had brought with him his small ship's cannon, which was mounted on an improvised carriage made from a wagon-axle, and at least one, and perhaps two, further cannon.

Pretorius' expedition set out from the Boer encampments moving north, crossing the high plateau west of the Mzinyathi River before descending to cross the river north of the later-named Rorke's Drift and moving into the open valley of the Ncome River. As Pretorius' scouts suggested that he was about to enter a grassy landscape largely free of bush, he collected along the way sufficient wood to improvise *veghegte*, 'fighting gates', with which to block up the gaps between the wagons.

The modern monument gives a good impression of the effective barricade provided by the *laager*. (Author)

The Trekkers' viewpoint, looking out over the open ground across which most of the Zulu attacks developed. In fact, the *veghegte*, or 'fighting gates' – improvised hurdles of wood – were less uniform than the monument suggests, but nonetheless were effective. (Author)

The progress of his advance was, of course, easily spotted by King Dingane's scouts, despite the Trekker habit of shooting any suspicious Zulu they found in their vicinity. It was clear that a significant clash was imminent, and during the second week of December, the king began to assemble and ritually prepare his *amabutho*. Still worried that the Port Natal settlers might make a demonstration of some sort, he mustered those *amabutho* quartered in the royal homesteads near the coast in their *amakhanda* there, and assembled his main striking arm at eMgungundlovu. It is difficult to be precise about its strength, but it probably numbered between 10,000 and 15,000 men and was placed under the command of both Ndlela kaSompisi

The view across the grassy flats towards the *laager* which faced most of the Zulus during the battle, with Vegkop behind. (Author)

Note: gridlines are shown at intervals of 500m (546.8 yards).

ZULU

1. Zulu left horn (iziThunyisa, uDlambedlu and imVokwe *amabutho*)
2. Zulu chest (iziNyosi and uDlangezwa *amabutho*)
3. Zulu right horn (izinGulutshane and umKhulutshane *amabutho*)
4. Zulu loins (reserve; uKhokhothi *ibutho*)

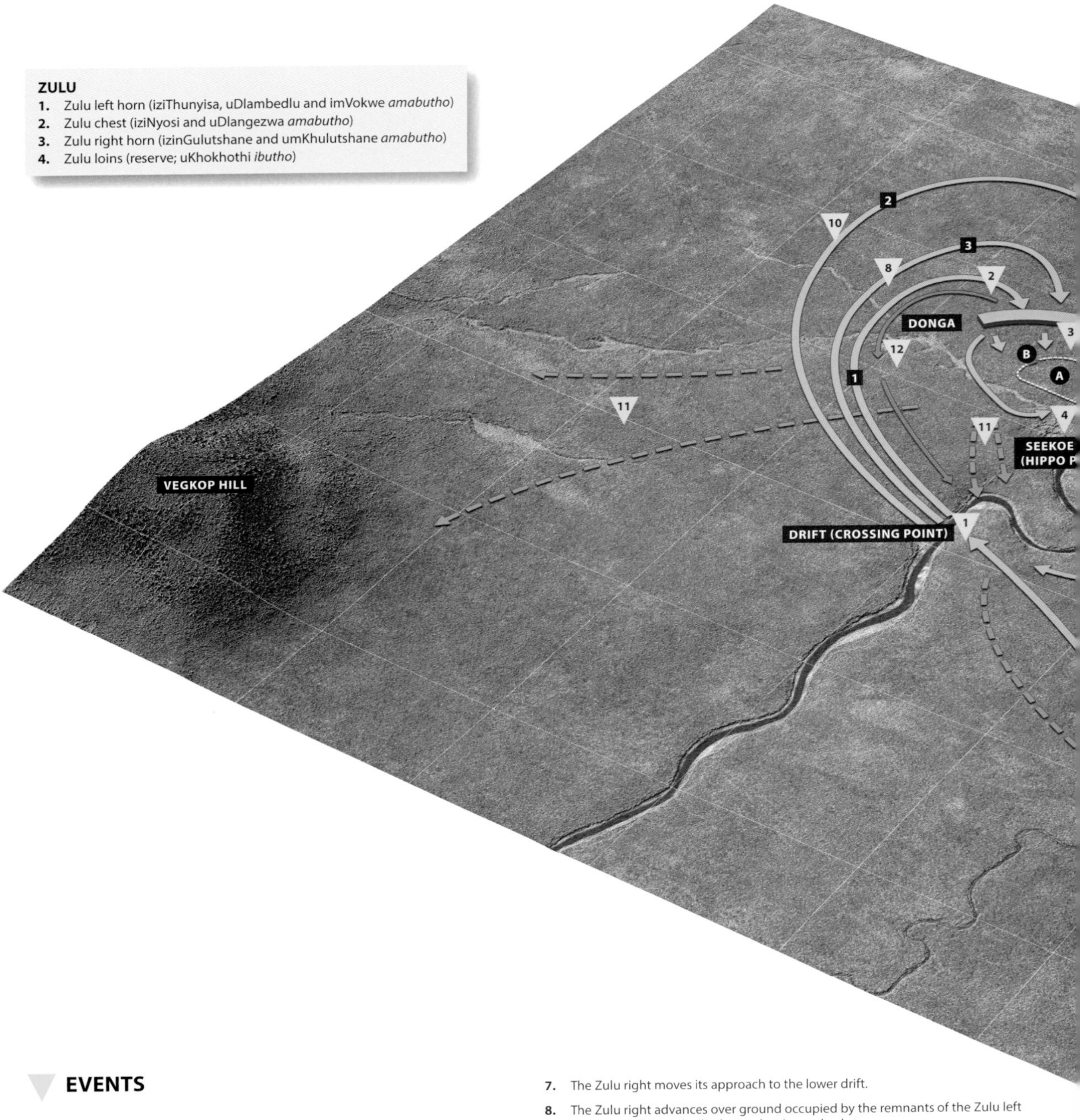

EVENTS

1. The Zulu left horn arrives on the battlefield in advance of the rest of the Zulu army, and moves to cross the drift below the *donga*.

2. The Zulu left deploys on the open ground between the *donga* and the river.

3. The Zulus attack the wagon *laager* repeatedly but are driven off with heavy losses.

4. Elements of the Zulu left occupy the *donga*. Here they become packed so tightly that they are unable to resist a Boer sortie which fires down into them from the banks above.

5. The Zulu right horn advances to the upper drift.

6. A Boer sortie from the *laager* disrupts the attempts by the Zulu right horn to cross the river, refusing the Zulus a foothold on the western bank.

7. The Zulu right moves its approach to the lower drift.

8. The Zulu right advances over ground occupied by the remnants of the Zulu left horn. It repeatedly attacks the *laager*, but is repulsed.

9. The Zulu chest approaches.

10. The Zulu chest attacks the *laager* across ground already occupied by the disrupted horns but after several attacks is repulsed.

11. The Zulus begin to retire away from the *laager* in confusion. Some Zulus retire to the slopes of Vegkop or retreat across the river.

12. A mounted Boer pursuit led by Pretorius breaks up the retreating Zulus and drives them away from the *laager*. It pursues them across the river, causing heavy casualties.

13. The Zulus rout away from the battlefield, offering little resistance to the Boers pursuing them.

THE BATTLE OF BLOOD RIVER/NCOME, 16 DECEMBER 1838, 0400–1300HRS

The view from the south-east, showing the position of the Boer *laager* on the banks of the river. The *laager* was carefully sited to restrict the Zulus' room to manoeuvre, particularly with regard to the limited crossing points on the river; this resulted in a series of uncoordinated and increasingly disorganized attacks over the same ground.

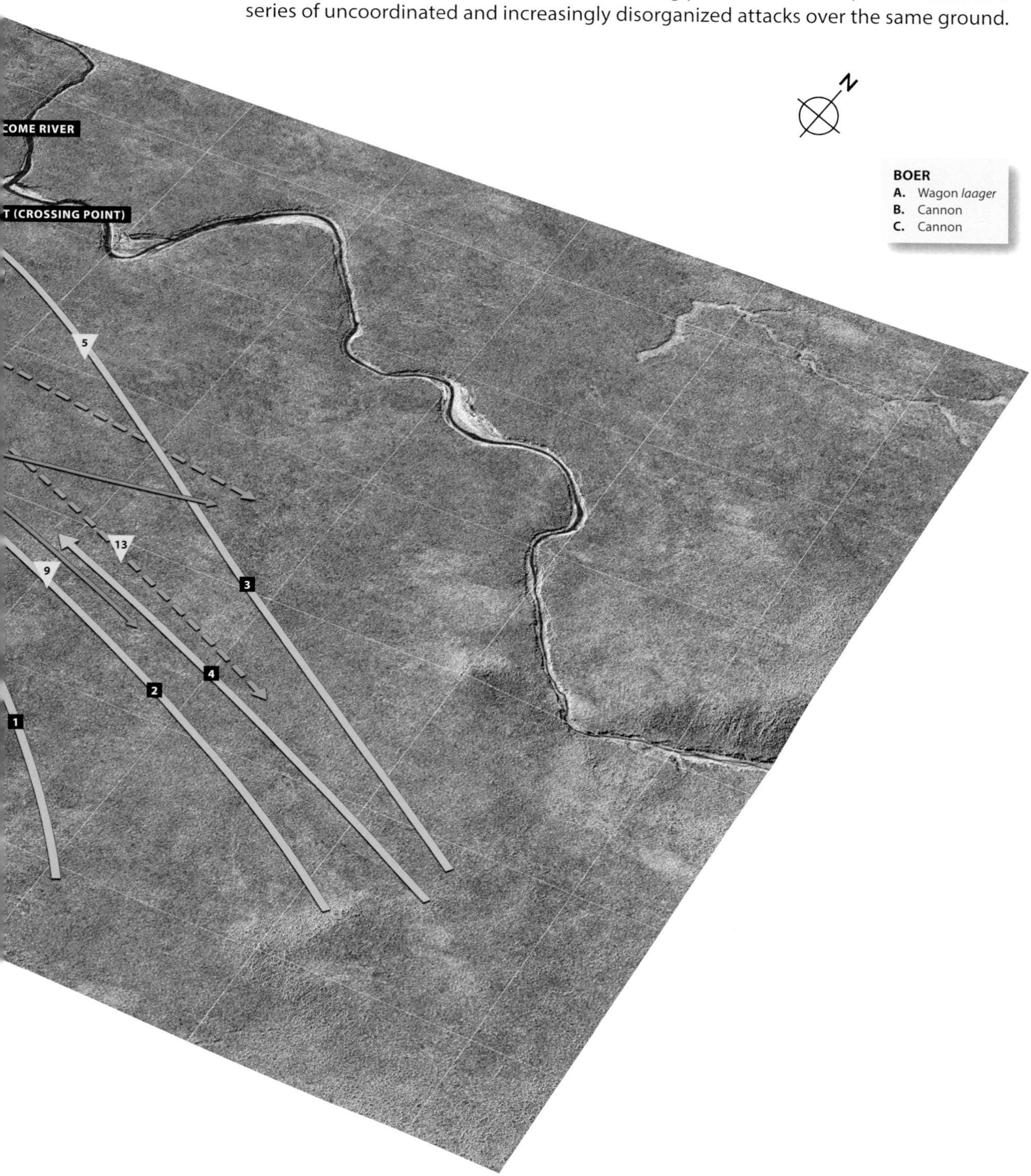

BOER
A. Wagon *laager*
B. Cannon
C. Cannon

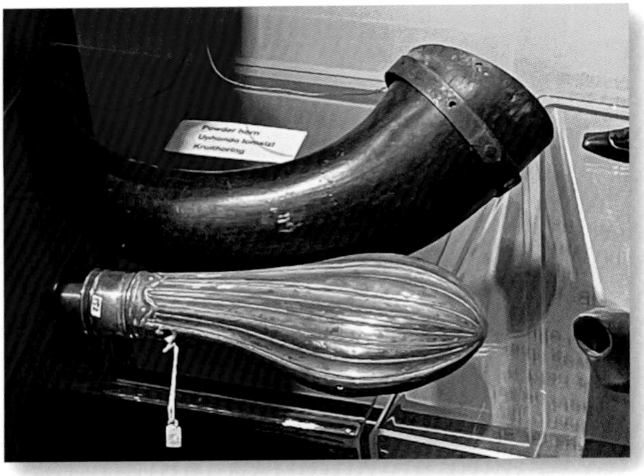

A Trekker powder horn and a rather more elegant powder flask in the Ncome Museum. (Author)

and Nzobo kaSobadli. The army set out around 12 December, moving westwards and hoping to intercept the *kommando* before it reached the Zulu heartland.

The Trekkers reached the west bank of the Ncome River on 15 December. A Trekker patrol crossed the river and scouted past a low range of hills beyond, returning to report that the Zulu army was approaching. By that time, the expedition's wagons had reached the river and some were preparing to cross, but Pretorius himself rode out and, having noted the Zulu strength for himself, returned and instructed that, rather than hurry across the river, a spot be selected for a *laager* on the near bank instead. The ground was an open, largely flat floodplain, framed on either side by a hill on the western bank – which the Boers were to call Vegkop, 'fight hill' – and two lower ridges, Nthabane and Shogane, on the far bank. The river itself was full and flowed lazily through a deep pool, where the Trekkers saw traces of hippopotamus and which they christened the *seekoeigat* ('sea-cow pool'). Along the banks of the pool, the ground was low-lying, marshy and covered in thick reeds, and there were serviceable drifts above and below the pool. A steep, narrow *donga* (erosion gully) roughly 10–20ft deep snaked down from Vegkop and into the river below the pool.

The exact position of Pretorius' *laager* has been contested, but the modern monument positions it 100 yards away from the river. Veterans of the battle later disagreed on its exact position, some placing it closer to the natural defences of the river but others arguing that the gap was left deliberately to draw the Zulus into a killing zone between the *laager* and the marshy pool. Either way, the *laager* was carefully constructed so that it nestled into the angle between the *donga* and the river itself. The wagon pole of each wagon was run under the one in front, and the gaps were filled with the pre-prepared *veghegte*. The livestock – some 1,400 oxen and horses – were corralled inside the circle, and to prevent them becoming a stampede hazard, the ox teams were kept yoked together, tied head-to-head in pairs

The walls of the Ncome Museum, built on the eastern banks of the river, over which the Zulus advanced, are designed to reflect the encircling 'horns of the beast' attack formation, and are faced by outsize representations of war shields. (Author)

'Ou Grietjie', one of the cannon which Pretorius brought to the *laager* mounted on an improvised carriage. (Author)

to restrict their movement; throughout the battle, the African drivers would kneel beside their charges, talking gently to them in an attempt to prevent them from panicking. That night, Pretorius instructed that lanterns be hung on the long drivers' whips and hung out over the wagons to provide a narrow pool of light around the *laager* to prevent a surprise attack. The cannon were placed in gaps between the wagons facing the open plain on the other sides from the river and *donga*. That evening, Sarel Celliers once again led the expedition in prayers and repeated their commitment to their vow.

Both Ndlela and Nzobo were experienced commanders, but it seems their approach to the river was badly timed. Before dawn on the 16th, the Zulus approached in three columns, the central chest flanked on either side by the two horns. It seems, however, that the young men of the left horn – about 3,000 men of the uDlambedlu and imVokwe *amabutho*, screened by perhaps 200 men carrying muskets and mounted on captured horses, the newly formed iziThunyisa – had outstripped the body of the army and reached the river at the lower drift before dawn. A heavy mist lay in the valley, and little could be seen of the Trekker dispositions beyond an unnerving circle of light cast by the lanterns. Not waiting for the main body to support them – or indeed for Ndlela and Nzobo to assess the situation – the Zulu left crossed the river in the dark and silently moved across the *donga* to surround the *laager* on the open field to the north. There they sat down to await daylight.

Dawn broke, and by about 0630hrs the mist began to lift on a clear, bright, windless day, giving the Trekkers inside the *laager* their first unsettling sight of the left horn already in position to attack. As soon as it was light, the Zulus rose up, drummed their spears on their shields and ran straight at the wagons. As they reached within 20–30 yards of

There were at least two small cannon within the *laager*, possibly three. There is a story that a shot from one caused the Zulu commanders on the hills on the far side of the river to duck – but the story postdates the battle and may be apocryphal. (Author)

A replica of '*Ou Grietjie*', one of the Trekker cannon used in the battle, is fired at the Blood River/Ncome Visitors' Centre in 2024. The cannon was a ship's carronade, mounted on a carriage improvised from wagon parts. The war with the Trekkers was the first time the Zulu army was exposed to European artillery. (Author)

the wagon-wall, the defenders opened fire, pouring a great barrage of shot and *lopers* into the Zulu ranks at close range. Pretorius had instructed his men to fire in groups, one section firing as another reloaded, thus keeping up a rolling fire, whilst the cannon fired canister shot improvised from musket balls and scrap metal. The shock of the fire was so great that the Zulus withdrew, only to regroup and charge again across a ground now littered with bodies. Although the iziThunyisa seem to have hung at a distance around the *laager*, they fired at too great a distance to be effective, thus proving to have no demonstrable effect on the battle whatsoever. After several attempts had proved equally unsuccessful, they began to hesitate, and their officers directed them instead to move past the southern face of the *laager* and pour into the *donga* on the southern side. This enabled them to get closer to the *laager* without being shot, but the banks were too steep to allow them to climb out easily and the *donga* soon became congested with a press of warriors who could hardly move. Pretorius, spotting his opportunity, called on volunteers to make a mounted sally. They rode out over the open ground covered by the first attacks, shooting the wounded Zulus, and lined the banks of the *donga*, firing down into the helpless warriors packed below. It was too much for the left horn, which began to disperse and drift away to the slopes of Vegkop to regroup.

By this time, the right horn and chest of the Zulu army could clearly be seen approaching on the flats across the river. The right horn, consisting of the umKhulutshane and izinGulutshane *amabutho*, moved upstream with the

The deep *donga* which flows to the south of the *laager*, and which Pretorius incorporated into his defences. Vegkop is behind. (Author)

Looking down the *donga* towards the river, with the *laager* on the left. The Zulu advance was across the plain in the far distance. (Author)

intention of encircling the *laager* to the north. Here they attempted to cross the river at the upper drift, above the hippo pool, but Pretorious saw them coming and his mounted men, still outside the *laager*, lined the bank and shot the Zulus down mid-stream. This was enough to cause the right horn to abandon the crossing, and instead they followed the river downstream, crossing at the same lower drift where the left horn had done so earlier.

Seeking shelter from the curtain of fire which surrounded the *laager* to the north, elements of the left horn occupied the *donga*, only to find themselves trapped by its steep banks. (Author)

THE ZULU ATTACK AT BLOOD RIVER/NCOME, 16 DECEMBER 1838 (PP.68–69)

The start of the main phase of the battle, as the right horn of the Zulu army (**1**), the umKhulutshane and izinGulutshane *amabutho*, cross the *donga* (**2**) south of the Boer *laager* on their way to attack. The left horn (**3**), seen here in the distance, had already approached by the same route before dawn that morning and mounted several attacks on the open ground to the north of the *laager*. Pretorius' careful placing of the wagon circle (**4**) had severely restricted the Zulu movements, however. After unsuccessfully assaulting the *laager*, some elements of the Zulu left had occupied this *donga* in the hope that it would protect them from the Trekker fire; in the event, it proved a death trap as the warriors, once in it, were too congested to fight and were exposed to the fire of Boer sorties lining the banks above them. By the time the right horn approached, the Zulu attacks were already becoming confused, and each new *ibutho* to arrive on the field was forced to pass through the ranks of those already there. The attacks by the Zulu left were accompanied by musketry from the iziThunyisa (**5**), a small detachment of Zulus mounted on captured Boer horses and carrying captured Boer muskets; there is no suggestion, however, that the iziThunyisa made any significant contribution to the attacks. These attacks would be repeated throughout the morning as fresh *amabutho* from the Zulu chest, advancing across the plain in the distance (**6**), were fed into battle. Despite considerable Zulu gallantry, however, the *laager*'s defences were never penetrated.

The height of the battle, as the Zulus repeatedly attack the *laager*. (Author)

They advanced through the trampled grass and the dead and dying men left by the earlier attacks, and began to attack over the same open stretch of ground. They, too, were met by a destructive fire at close range, and had no more luck than the left horn. Behind them, as they continued their futile assaults, the chest – men of the iziNyosi and uDlangezwa *amabutho* – had also crossed the river and was manoeuvring into position. The battlefield was now increasingly congested, and the chest had to advance through the lines of the progressively demoralized right horn, the newcomers indignantly pushing the men ahead of them out of the way in their effort to reach the front ranks. Yet the older men of the chest were no more successful than those in the horns had been, and the morning dissolved into a series of increasingly uncoordinated attacks, which tested the endurance of both the attackers and defenders alike. Sometimes the attacks were so intense that the Trekkers had no time to ram down their powder and shot, simply pouring them into the barrel, thumping the butt of the musket hard upon the ground, then pointing the muzzle into the clouds of smoke surrounding the wagons and pulling the trigger.

By noon, the Zulu attacks had become completely uncoordinated, and with no apparent hope of breaching the *laager*'s defences, some of the *amabutho* began to regroup with the obvious intention of withdrawing. Pretorius, realizing this was his moment to completely disrupt the Zulu army, gathered 160 of his men who mounted up, leaving the rest to guard the *laager*. A wagon was dragged aside and the Trekkers emerged from the northern face of the *laager*. Splitting into two parties, they turned left and right, shooting any wounded Zulus on the ground or those trying to hide in holes or *dongas*, and herding the rest towards the two drifts either side of the hippo pool. Many of the Zulus scattered, but those who tried to remain with their *amabutho* crowded at the drifts, where the Trekkers fired into the mass of them. Many warriors threw themselves into the river and tried to hide among the reeds, lying under the water with just their noses protruding. Some Boers dismounted and painstakingly stalked them, shooting them down as

INSIDE THE *LAAGER* AT BLOOD RIVER/NCOME, 16 DECEMBER 1838 (PP.72–73)

The battle of Blood River/Ncome demonstrated that, if properly managed, the defensive *laager* formation was almost invulnerable to attacks made by men armed only with close-quarter weapons. At Blood River, Andries Pretorius had perhaps perfected the art of the *laager*; the wagons were closely drawn together, with improvised wooden gates used to block the gaps between them (**1**). The Trekkers took up a position between the wagons (**2**) or underneath them (**3**), and were able to lay down a devastating curtain of fire at close range which prevented the Zulus from getting near enough to use their stabbing spears. Also shown in the plate are a detachment of African musketeers from the Port Natal settlement who, led by Alexander Biggar, had joined the Boer expedition (**4**). The role of African participants on the Trekker side is often overlooked, but not only did the Natal musketeers add their firepower to the defences, but the role of African wagon drivers and ox-team leaders was essential in calming the huge herd of horses and oxen confined within the *laager*. Here, a *Voorlooper* – a team-leader – is calming two teams of yoked oxen who have been tied head-to-head to restrict their movement (**5**). The dress of the Trekkers differed from the popular image of the late 19th-century Boer fighter; the Trekkers preferred to wear short jackets or waistcoats, straw hats were common, and powder was carried in horns attached to a waist belt. Each Trekker brought his own weapon, a variety of flintlock and percussion types, many of them firing *lopers*, small bags of shot which exploded on leaving the muzzle and were devastating on a closely packed target at short range.

An illustration from Adulphe Delagorgue's memoir of the campaign which conflates the two defining incidents of the war – the massacre of the Trekker encampments, right, and the victory at Blood River, left. (DeAgostini/Getty Images)

they lay helpless. Once across the river, all semblance of order disintegrated and the Zulus fled headlong across the flats, many too exhausted to resist when the Boers rode near, although Pretorius himself had a narrow escape when one warrior turned to stab him, pulling him from his horse. Pretorius managed to catch the blade, cutting his hand, and the two were wrestling when another Trekker came past and shot the Zulu.

Pretorius called off the pursuit as the last Zulu bands disappeared over the Shogane hills. The plain on both sides of the river was littered with Zulu dead, and so many were killed in the hippo pool that it looked like a sluggish pool of blood. Thereafter, the Trekkers remembered the battle by the name *Bloedrivier* – Blood River.

After the battle, Pretorius assessed the Zulu casualties at not less than 3,000 men. This was perhaps an overestimate – in comparable battles between British troops armed with breach-loading rifles and modern artillery and the Zulu army during the Anglo-Zulu War of 1879, Zulu casualties seldom numbered 2,000 men, even after several hours of fighting – but there was no doubt they had suffered heavily. In return, not one

The climax of the battle, with the Zulus retreating across the river in disarray, pursued by the victorious Trekkers. (Painting by W. H. Coetzee/Author)

In a frieze sculpted in the first stone monument on the battlefield, Pretorius rides out at the head of his victorious *kommando* to smite the retreating Zulus. (Author)

of the Trekkers had been killed and only three were wounded, including Pretorius himself.

So great did their victory seem that the Trekkers believed God had accepted their vow and granted them the decisive action they had so long yearned for.

THE BATTLE OF oPATHE

Although the victory on the banks of the Ncome had undoubtedly inflicted great damage on the Zulu army, the Trekkers were keen to carry the war all the way to King Dingane himself, and once they had recovered from their exertions Pretorius ordered the expedition to press on to eMgungundlovu. The Zulus were in no position to resist, and instead King Dingane decided to abandon his principal homestead and put it to the torch. Pretorius arrived at eMgungundlovu on the 20th to find it a great circle of burnt-out and smouldering huts; his men picked about the ruins, and on the slopes of

The battlefield of oPathe, looking up the valley down which Bhongoza lured the Trekker *kommando*; the initial ambush took place about halfway down. In December 1838, after heavy summer rains, the countryside would have been much greener. (Brandyne Arendse)

The battle of oPathe, 27 December 1838

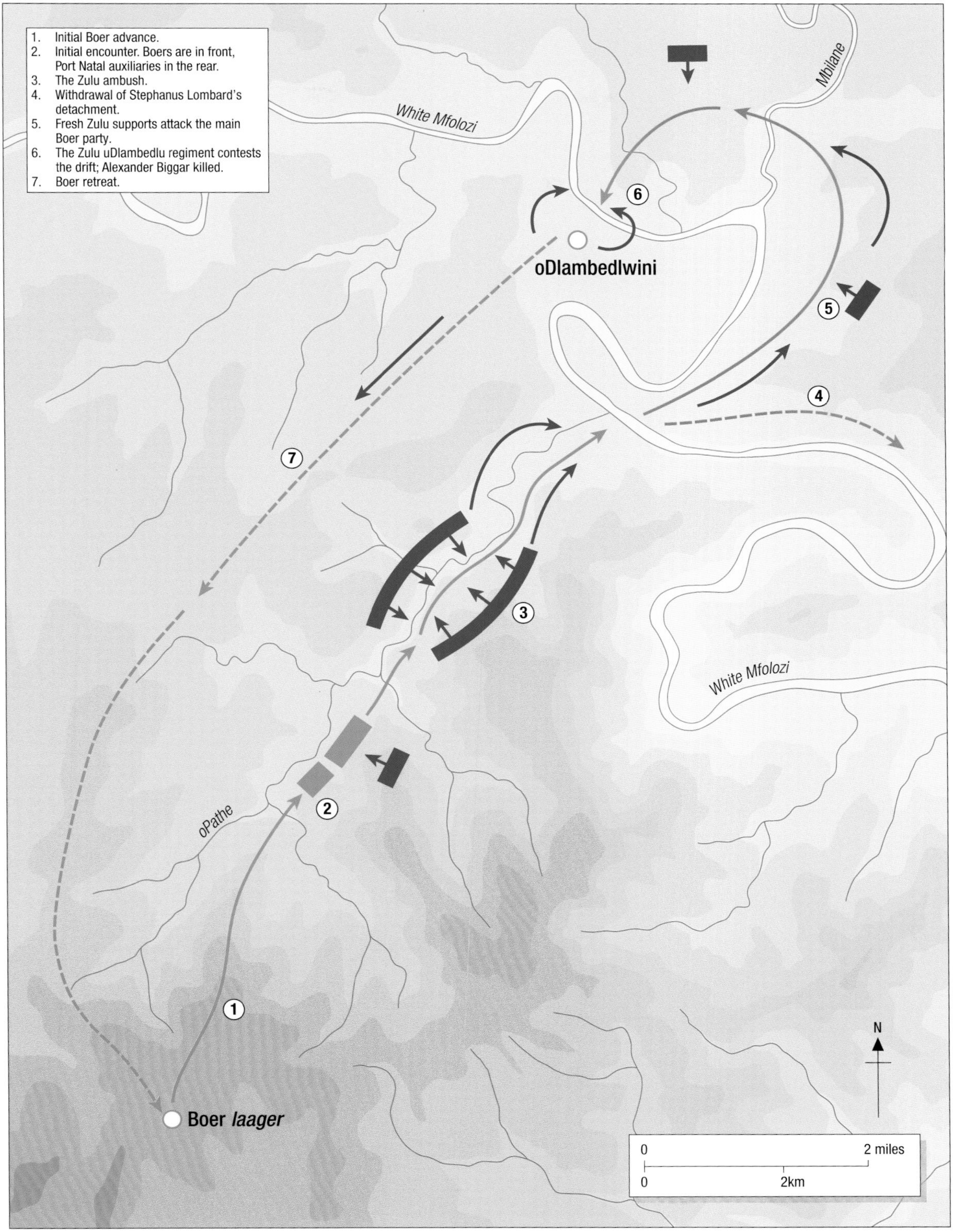

Looking from the upper end of the oPathe valley towards the White Mfolozi River. The Trekkers were attacked on the way down, but rather than try to retreat they fought their way through the Zulu cordon and a running battle developed down and across the river. (Brandyne Arendse)

Alexander Biggar, sketched as an officer of the 85th Regiment. Biggar had the most military experience of the Port Natal settlers, and he lost two sons during the early stages of the war. He commanded a contingent of African musketeers at both Blood River and oPathe, where he was killed. (Author)

KwaMatiwane they found the remains of Piet Retief and his men, which they gathered up and buried. They were still in the area a few days later when they captured a suspected spy, a man named Bhongoza kaMefu. Under interrogation, Bhongoza told them that the king had fled, but that in his haste he had abandoned thousands of head of royal cattle on the plain beyond the White Mfolozi River. The Trekkers moved their camp westwards from eMgungundlovu, onto the Mthonjaneni heights, which gave them a commanding view of the White Mfolozi valley – and here they allowed themselves to be persuaded by Bhongoza's story. Pretorius himself, nursing his wounded hand, opted to remain behind but, on the 27th, 300 mounted men under Karel Landman and Hans Dons de Lange, accompanied by Alexander Biggar and his African auxiliaries, and led by Bhongoza with a rope around his neck, descended into the valley to capture the king's cattle. Bhongoza led them down the steep and narrow oPathe valley, pointing out far ahead the apparent signs of cattle on the plain.

The 'cattle' were in fact warriors crouched behind their shields. Although the *amabutho* who had fought at Ncome were dispirited, Dingane had managed to rally enough of them to continue their defiance, and Bhongoza was leading them into a carefully prepared trap. Midway down the valley, the track passed through a narrow defile, and as the Boers entered it, a voice called out loudly in isiZulu, 'They are surrounded, men of the

The spot on the White Mfolozi where Biggar and most of his men were killed. They were retreating from the left, but the oDlambedlwini royal homestead was on the flats on the right, and the retreat was cut off by members of the uDlambedlu *ibutho*. (Brandyne Arendse)

King!' Bhongoza managed to slip away in the confusion, and the Trekkers suddenly found themselves showered with throwing spears from both sides of the gorge. Karel Landman wanted to dismount and fight, but Hans De Lange urged instead that they try to break through the Zulu cordon by pressing forward. They rode down the defile, closely pressed on all sides, and with Biggar's auxiliaries on foot running behind. Ahead of them lay the White Mfolozi River, and as they drew near its banks, they managed to break through the Zulu lines. Once across the river, however, in more open country, they found themselves pressed by another Zulu force coming up from their right. A party of some 50 men under Stephanus Lombard broke away and rode off to the east – they eventually returned safely to the Trekker camp on Mthonjaneni – but the rest turned west, following the river upstream. Here they reached a drift across the river and, still hard pressed by the pursing Zulus, turned to cross it. Just across the river lay the oDlambedlwini royal homestead, where the uDlambedlu *ibutho* were waiting to join the fray. The Zulus rushed forward to occupy the crossing, stabbing at the Boers as they tried to fight their way through. Most of the Boers on horseback managed to extricate themselves, but Alexander Biggar's men, on foot and exhausted, were caught and trapped; Biggar, the former professional soldier, opted to stay with his men, and most of them were killed along the water's edge.

De Lange and Landman managed to keep their men together, despite a persistent pursuit, as they rode away from the White Mfolozi valley. Five of the Trekkers were killed and many more wounded, and most of the Port Natal contingent was wiped out – far more casualties than the Trekkers had suffered during the entire battle of Blood River. Although the Zulu losses were probably heavy, they had driven the Trekkers off with ignominy and had remained in possession of the field, capturing dozens of abandoned muskets and horses.

The expedition would prove to be the last major clash between the Trekkers and Zulus in the war, and gave the lie to the assumption that Blood River/Ncome had been a decisive victory.

THE BATTLE OF amaQONGQO AND THE END OF THE WAR

In the aftermath of the fighting of December 1838, both sides drew apart. It was clear to Pretorius that, while Blood River had delivered a severe defeat, the Zulu army had not been destroyed, and it was impossible for the Trekkers to maintain their position in central Zululand. Instead, the *kommando* withdrew to the encampments in the uKhahlamba foothills and set about creating a new republic south of the Thukela River – the Republic of Natalia – and a new capital, Pietermaritzburg, was laid out in the Natal midlands. Port Natal did not come under its authority since the British, concerned about the volatile situation in Natal, had moved a small garrison to occupy the port in defence of the settlers' prior claim to the area – although with the war apparently over, the governor of the Cape increasingly saw the British presence there as an expensive irrelevance.

King Dingane, meanwhile, did not attempt to return to his eMgungundlovu homestead, but instead moved north and established a new capital – also called eMgungundlovu – on the Vuna River. From here, he tentatively opened negotiations with the Trekkers to formally end the hostilities, and eventually agreed to acknowledge their claim to the territory south of the Thukela and to pay reparations in cattle.

In fact, the king, realizing that the Trekkers were likely to remain uneasy neighbours, planned to shift the focus of his kingdom further north still into the country beyond the Phongolo River. This area was controlled by the Swazi kingdom, but Dingane was confident that his army, despite the losses inflicted by the Boers, was still significantly stronger than the Swazi forces. He was also aware that the Swazi strategy in previous clashes was to avoid a direct confrontation and retire to natural strongholds rather than risk a military defeat. In the middle of 1839, Zulu *amabutho* were despatched to build a new homestead north of the Phongolo River as a clear assertion of ownership. This was too much of a challenge for the Swazi king, Sobhuza, who mobilized his own forces to drive out the Zulus. In late 1839, the two sides met in an unusually pitched battle on the Lobuye River – and after fierce but inconclusive fighting, the Swazis generally had the better of things, but no decisive victory was achieved.

The failure of his Swazi expedition not only checked King Dingane's northern ambitions but irrevocably damaged his already tarnished prestige among his own people, precipitating a split in the kingdom which finally brought about his own downfall and an end to the conflict with the Voortrekkers. In September 1839, just months after the Swazi setback, Prince Mpande kaSenzangakhona crossed the Thukela with some 17,000 followers and established a new homestead at Thongathi, 25 miles north of Port Natal. Prince Mpande had been a significant figure in the southern part of the Zulu kingdom, and had been the nominal commander of the expedition that had defeated the settlers at the battle of the Thukela. He was an astute political survivor who masked a keen political brain behind an air of indolence and indifference, which had allowed him to survive court intrigues since the days of King Shaka. After the Swazi campaign, however, Mpande had become increasingly convinced that Dingane was suspicious of his allegiance, and indeed it is possible that Mpande had been carefully building links to Zululand's great regional *amakhosi* (chiefs). Taking advantage of

The battle of amaQongqo, 29 January 1840

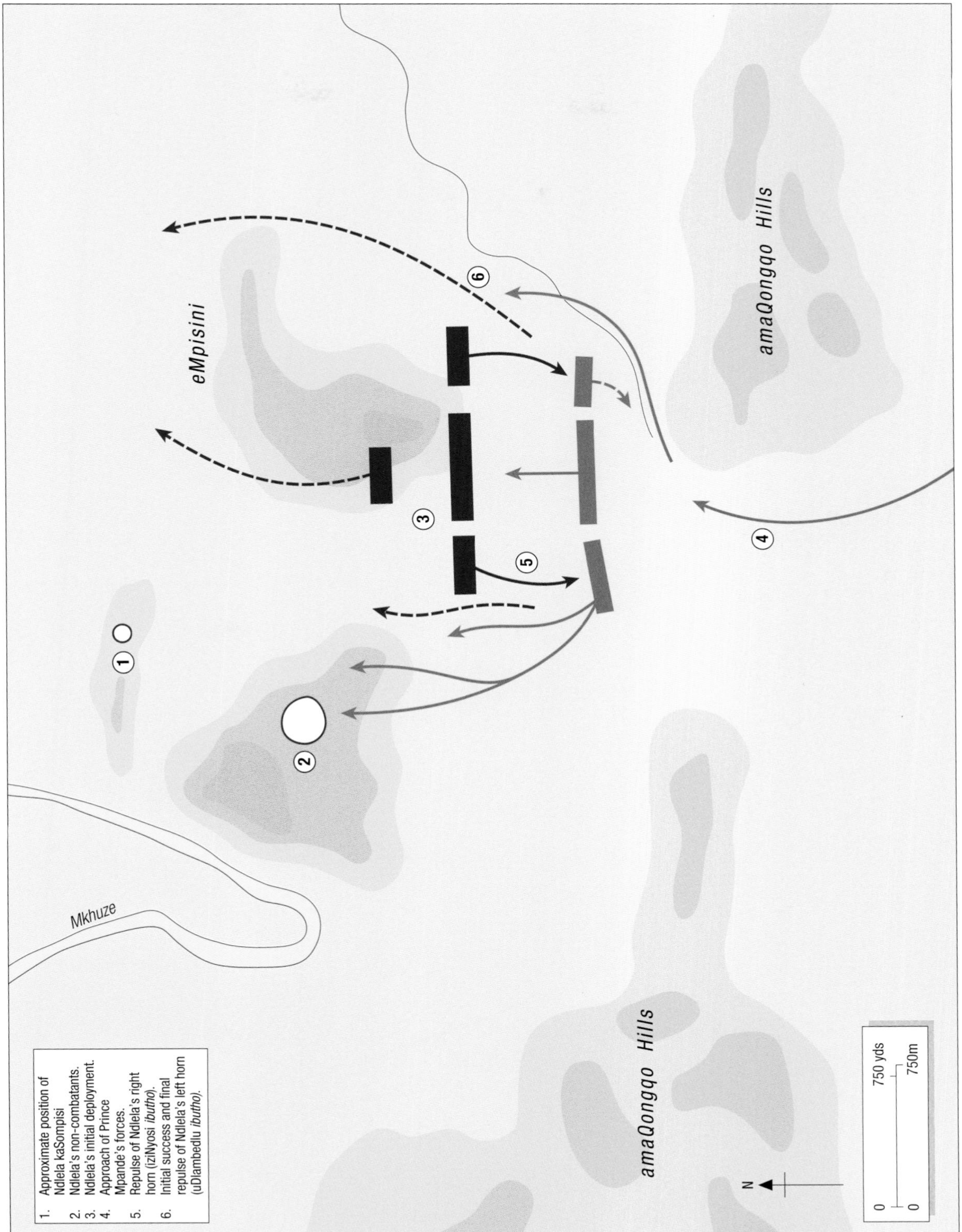

Prince Mpande negotiating with Trekker envoys; it was Mpande's decision to break away from King Dingane which facilitated the Trekker victory in a long-running and bloody conflict. (Author)

the king's dwindling control, Mpande had simply moved himself beyond Dingane's reach.

The Voortrekkers were initially disturbed by this wholesale migration of a section of the Zulu kingdom, until it occurred to them that an alliance with a legitimate member of the Zulu Royal House afforded them a fresh opportunity to resolve their quarrel with Dingane. In October 1839, the Trekkers offered to support Mpande in an offensive against the king. Both parties were reluctant to act while there were British troops stationed at Port Natal, but the British garrison was withdrawn in December, leaving the Trekkers free to pursue their plans without interference. The Trekkers repudiated their peace treaty with King Dingane on the basis that he had failed to supply all the agreed reparations, and they resumed the war in the middle of January 1840.

The plan was that Prince Mpande's followers would advance directly north from Thongathi to Dingane's new eMgungundlovu while Andries Pretorius

A bas-relief sculpture in the Voortrekker Monument in Pretoria depicting the accord between Prince Mpande and the Natal Trekkers which paved the way for the final stage of the Trekker war against King Dingane in January 1840. (Author)

would lead a *kommando* north from the Trekker settlements in central Natal. Pretorius' *kommando* consisted of 308 Trekkers, 500 *agterryers* and wagon drivers, and 50 wagons; Mpande's force consisted of all the fighting men who had defected with him, many of whom were members of the *amabutho* quartered in the southern part of the country, and whom Mpande had given into the command of Nongalaza kaNondela, his senior *induna* at the battle of Thukela. To distinguish themselves from Dingane's forces, Mpande's warriors adopted a field badge as a sign of their allegiance, with two long strips of white cowhide hanging over the chest and back.

Mpande – as king – reviewing his army in the 1840s. Despite an indolent manner, Prince Mpande was an astute political survivor, a veteran of the battle of the Thukela, who emerged as the true victor of the Trekker–Zulu War. (Author)

Pretorius' advance was hampered by heavy rain and swollen rivers, and it was Nongalaza's forces who reached King Dingane first. Dingane had placed his usual general, Ndlela kaSompisi, in command of the roughly 5,000 troops who had remained loyal to him, and Ndlela had taken up position along a line of *kopjes* known as the amaQongqo hills near the Mkhuze River. On 29 January, Nongalaza's *impi* approached the hills, and both sides formed up in traditional battle array. The king, convinced that Mpande's men would not have the stomach for a determined fight, instructed Ndlela to mount a single determined attack, but Ndlela was more cautious and was determined to approach the battle with more flexibility. In the event, Ndlela began the battle by sending out his horns, with the uDlambedlu *ibutho* on the left and the iziNyosi on the right. Nongalaza responded by committing his own horns. He had placed the imiHaye *ibutho*, which was largely intact, on his left, and a mixed contingent of men from various *amabutho* who had defected to Mpande on his right. The imiHaye steadily drove back the iziNyosi, but the uDlambedlu prevailed on Nongalaza's less-cohesive right. As the two armies slowly pivoted on the battlefield, the respective chests entered the fray and the battle became one of fierce bouts of fighting punctuated by short withdrawals, regroupings and renewed attacks. One hero on King Dingane's side, a noted warrior named Nozitshada kaMagoboza, an officer in the uDlambedlu, single-handedly took on successive groups of young warriors sent against him until he stood alone among a pile of dead and dying enemies, his shield soggy with blood. In the end, he became so exhausted that he changed to stabbing with his other arm, until finally he invited the enemy to kill him but, in awe, they only dared approach him in a rush. The battle raged throughout the afternoon until finally the uDlambedlu began to withdraw, and Dingane's army disengaged and fell back.

Although Dingane's *amabutho* had retired in good order, it was clear that Nongalaza had won the battle – and without relying on the support of Pretorius' *kommando*. When Ndlela, who had been stabbed in the thigh during the retreat, returned to Dingane, the king was furious, blaming him for not having followed his orders and suspecting the Ndlela had secretly made a pact with Prince Mpande. He ordered that Ndlela be killed, and the man who had hitherto supervised the long campaign against the Voortrekkers was executed; in deference to his rank, he was not clubbed to death, but a hide rope was passed around his neck, held taught and beaten with sticks so that his neck broke.

It was immediately clear that King Dingane's power was finished. He drifted north, accompanied by a dwindling number of councillors, courtiers and warriors still loyal to him, until he decided to build a new royal homestead in the Lebombo mountains, on the borders of the Swazi country. Called eSankoleni, 'The Secluded Spot', it was a pale shadow of his former palaces. Here, he tried to regroup his followers but his presence was an irritation to the local Nyawo people, who gave their allegiance to the Swazi king. Early one morning in March – possibly the 15th – a small group of Nyawo and Swazi warriors sneaked into eSankoleni and surprised Dingane as he emerged from

Warriors skirmishing. In the end, King Dingane's defeat came about not through the direct agency of the Trekkers, but through a fierce traditional battle between Zulu *amabutho*. (Author)

his hut. There was a brief scuffle in which Dingane was stabbed but managed to stagger off into the bush before the attackers fled. The king's warriors, rallying to his aid, found him in the bush, a deep wound in his thigh that had passed through to his stomach. He was carried back to his hut, where his wound was judged to be fatal, and he died shortly afterwards. According to some accounts, his own doctors hastened his end to prevent his suffering.

The news of his death was greeted with relief by both the Trekkers and Prince Mpande. For the Trekkers, it brought to a close their long and bitter struggle for Natal – by far the bloodiest episode in the whole Great Trek – and finally gave them the opportunity to enjoy the rich farming lands they had coveted. Pretorius honoured his agreement with Mpande, recognizing him as Dingane's rightful successor, the new King of the Zulu, although the compensation he demanded for his participation in the amaQongqo campaign was extortionate, insisting that Mpande give over not merely the land south of the Thukela but all that stretching north as far as the Black Mfolozi River.

In the end, it soon became clear that the Trekkers were simply too few to absorb such a huge tract of territory, and Mpande was able to establish his new royal homestead, kwaNodwengo, north of the White Mfolozi, not far from the oPathe battlefield, in an area he had nominally ceded to the Trekkers. From here, he patiently set about restoring the fortunes of the Royal House, coaxing back many of Dingane's scattered supporters, forming new *amabutho* and building new *amakhanda*.

AFTERMATH

Today, King Dingane's legacy is ambivalent. He is regarded by many Zulus as a hero who attempted to defend his country against the Trekker invaders, but whose strategies proved deeply destructive to the nation. A modern sculpture at the Ncome Museum. (Author)

THE EFFECTS OF THE WAR

For the Trekkers, their success in the war proved illusory and the Republic of Natalia was short-lived. It proved impossible for the Trekkers to control the land that Mpande had ceded them, and no attempt was made by them to settle the land north of the Thukela River. Large tracts of land within the republic were settled by African groups, many of whom were gradually returning to historic homelands now that the threat from the Zulu Royal House had been checked. For the Trekkers the cattle wealth and influence of these groups was challenging, and the republic sought to reduce these groups and bring them tightly under its control. This, and the potential to open unchallenged contact with rival world powers by way of Port Natal, reawakened the latent British fears that their presence was a destabilizing one across the region and prompted the British to reassert their claims to the port. In early 1842, a detachment of British troops was marched overland from their garrisons on the Cape Frontier, and on 4 May, the Union flag was raised over the settlement in the Bay of Natal. The Trekkers, determined not to find themselves under British rule again, demanded the troops withdraw, and a new and bizarre conflict took place at Port Natal. The British made a moonlight sortie from their camp to attack Boer settlements on the night of 23 May, but the Trekkers spotted their approach and ambushed them as they marched across the open beach. The British were defeated and hurried back to their camp, which the Boers promptly besieged. One of the British settlers, Dick King – who had survived the battle of the Thukela – slipped through the Boer lines and, with his Zulu servant Ndongeni, rode to the Cape Frontier to raise the alarm. Reinforcements sailed up the coast

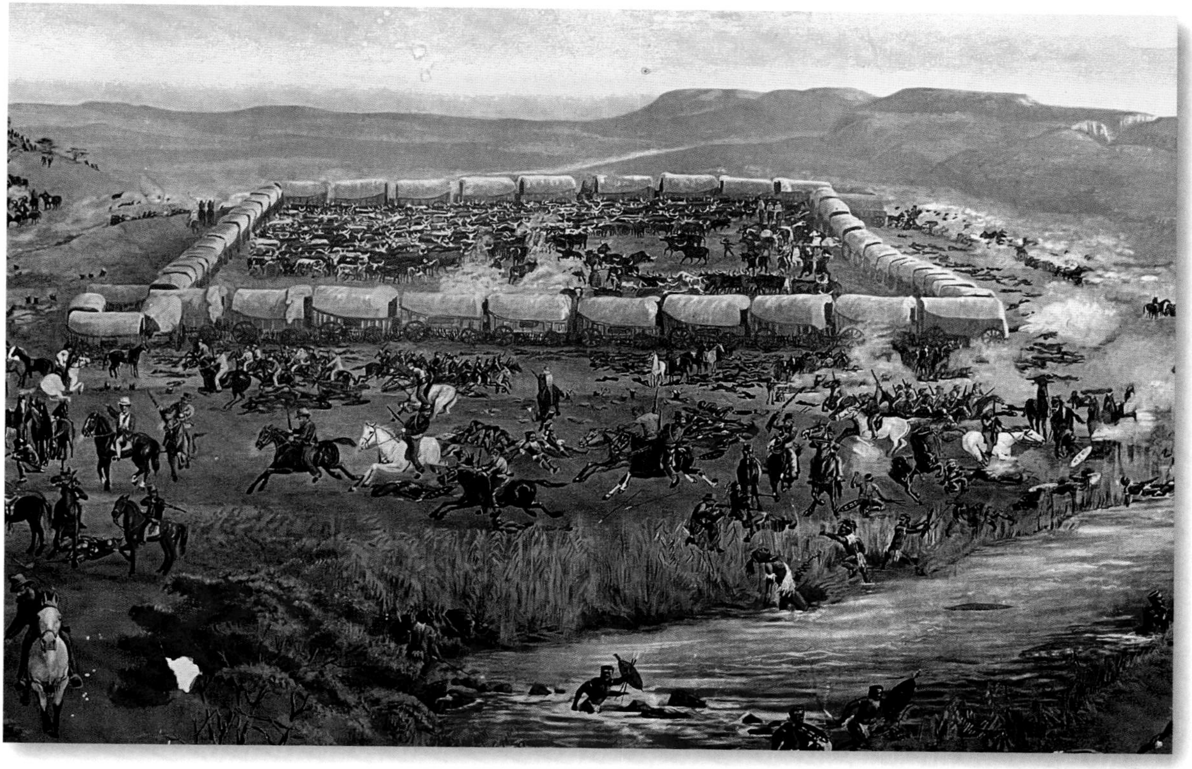

and landed under covering fire from a Royal Navy warship on 25 June. The Boer siege collapsed and the Trekkers reluctantly submitted to Queen Victoria. In May 1844, the Republic of Natalia was formally dissolved and Natal became a British colony. Many of those Trekkers who had travelled so far and struggled so hard to win the country abandoned it, and trekked back over the uKhahlamba to settle instead in the Transvaal. Although the dream of a Trekker republic in Natal had failed, the British formally recognized the independence of the inland republics (the Orange Free State and Transvaal) in 1853 and the Trekkers finally achieved something of their original objectives – a land free of British interference.

A lithograph published to mark the centenary of the battle of Blood River in 1938. It depicts the final stage of the battle and emphasizes the killing of retreating Zulus in the river which gave the battle its name. (Author)

With the arrival of the British, King Mpande was able to renegotiate his boundaries, reclaiming much of the land notionally ceded to the Trekkers and establishing the southern boundaries of Zululand along the line of the Mzinyathi and Thukela rivers. Only in the far north-west of the kingdom, where it abutted the Transvaal Republic, would there be any future territorial disputes, and the integrity of the Zulu kingdom remained intact until the Anglo-Zulu War of 1879. There is no doubt that King Dingane's war with the Trekkers had brought the Zulu kingdom to the brink of collapse, costing the lives of thousands of warriors, impoverishing the country through loss of cattle and severely damaging the structures of the state that King Shaka had built. The great royal homestead at eMgungundlovu, which had served King Dingane as a showcase for the country's wealth and power, had been destroyed, and the prestige of the monarchy had been badly damaged by the rift between Dingane and Mpande. Many of the regional *amakhosi* took the opportunity afforded by the rift to reassert some of the authority they had enjoyed before being

Envoys from King Mpande negotiate with the newly installed British Commissioner in Natal after the collapse of the Trekker Republic of Natalia and the imposition of British rule; the arrival of the British allowed Mpande to escape the restrictions of the treaties he had previously entered into with Andries Pretorius, and marked his emergence as the only real winner of the conflict of 1838–40. (Author).

subject to the Royal House. All of this afforded challenges which would dominate King Mpande's reign; and yet the same astute political sense which had seen him survive both King Shaka and King Dingane's reigns saw him patiently rebuild the kingdom, reinvigorating the damaged *amabutho* system, and slowly re-establishing central authority. Despite a damaging succession dispute in the 1850s, King Mpande would rule until 1872, the only one of the great Zulu kings of the 19th century to die peacefully of old age, and the kingdom he bequeathed to his son, Cetshwayo, was still robust enough to challenge British expansionism in 1879.

THE BATTLEFIELDS TODAY

The battle of Blood River/Ncome has remained contentious, the subject of intense political and ideological debate, a fact represented in the interpretation of the battlefield itself. The site of Pretorius' *laager* was originally marked with a cairn, supposedly in the centre of the wagon circle, although even veterans of the battle did not entirely agree on the spot. Although the Afrikaners lost the independence of their republics following the Anglo-Boer War of 1899–1902, their position began to recover with the merging of the Cape, Natal, Free State and Transvaal into the Union of South Africa in 1910. Afrikaner nationalism rose steadily from the advent of the centenary of the Great Trek in 1938, and Blood River achieved an iconic status as a defining moment in not only the history of the Trek movement but of right-wing Afrikaner ideology where it offered religious justification, through the vow made by the Trekkers beforehand, for the oppressive policies of the apartheid era. In 1947, a large stone monument in the form of a Trek wagon, with bas-relief panels celebrating the vow and Pretorius' victory, was placed on the site of the original marker cairn. During the height of the Nationalist Party's rule in 1971, it was decided to move this monument a few hundred yards away from the site of the *laager* and to replace it with a much more impressive statement celebrating the Trekker's great military triumph. It was decided to replace the stone monument with a life-sized recreation of the *laager* itself and, despite differences in contemporary accounts regarding the numbers present, some 64 wagons and three light cannon were cast in bronzed iron and arranged on the battlefield. The old cairn was used as a point of reference for placing the *laager* but there remains some debate as to whether it is in the correct spot, however, since although it aligns to the *donga* occupied by the Zulus during the battle, it is some distance from the Ncome river. Although the

The stone monument, first erected on the battlefield after the celebrations for the centenary of the Great Trek in 1938, originated on the site of the *laager* and was moved in 1973 to the periphery of the battlefield. It now stands outside the Trekker interpretation centre. (Author)

The battlefield viewed from the direction of the Zulu approach, with the distinctive outline of Vegkop beyond. The river flows through the centre of the photograph, marked by the clump of trees; a modern bridge spans the river to the right, and the reconstructed *laager* lies just above it. This is the view which the Zulu *impi* would have had on approaching the Trekker positions, and their movements were hampered by the availability of crossing points across the river. At the close of the battle they routed across this same ground, and suffered heavy casualties from the Trekker pursuit. (Author)

Ncome runs through shallow banks in a wide floodplain, it does not seem to have changed its course since 1838, and indeed traces of the old hippo pool, which Pretorius exploited as an obstacle to limit the Zulu approach, can still be seen. If the placing of the monument is correct the only viable explanation is that Pretorius deliberately allowed some space between the *laager* and the river in which to tempt the Zulus into a killing ground. Regardless, the current monument undoubtedly possesses a terrific presence, and an interpretation centre was built nearby to present the Trekker version of events. As recently as 2023 a walkway was added from the Trekker interpretation centre to the *laager*, with information boards offering key points of historical interest.With the collapse of the apartheid regime, however, it was decided to diffuse the triumphant iconography of the site and to reflect the importance of the site in the history of the Zulu kingdom, too, and a new interpretation centre on the east bank of the river – built on the ground over which the Zulus advanced – was opened in 1998. Designed to represent the sweeping curves of the Zulu 'chest and horns' attack formation, this is fronted by large metal representations of Zulu war shields, which face the *laager* across the river. The building includes interpretative displays on Zulu life during the reign of King Dingane. In between the two monuments, the Ncome River flows through low-lying, marshy ground, much as it did in December 1838, and the deep *dongas* which framed the *laager* remain a conspicuous feature of the site. In the open flats around the *laager*, where the Zulu *amabutho* once jostled for position, the thigh-length grass ripples gently in the breeze.

Of the other sites connected to the conflict, that of King Dingane's eMgungundlovu royal homestead is the best preserved. When the Zulus abandoned and set fire to the complex after Blood River, the heat from the burning thatch baked many of the hut floors to brick, and several of these have remained intact across 180 years. They are now preserved by a team of

The view towards the *laager* from the north-west; Pretorius deliberately channelled the Zulu approach to leave them with few options but to launch repeated assaults across this constricted space. (Author)

archaeologists, and some of the huts in the *isigodlo* area – the king's private preserve – have been reconstructed over the original floors. On a low rocky knoll opposite, KwaMatiwane, the graves of Piet Retief and his followers are marked with large stone monuments.

Of the Trekker encampments in the uKhahlamba foothills, the site at Veglaer is now beneath the waters of a dam, while monuments mark the sites and graves associated with other *laagers*, but some are in poor repair on land that is difficult to access. A small village, established by the Trekkers after the war, stands in the centre of the area attacked in February 1838 and named to commemorate the lost of so many women and children, is still called Weenen – 'weeping'. Towards the coast, the site of the battlefield of the Thukela is now under heavy sugar-cane cultivation. The hill above the 'Ndondakusuka homesteads is marked by a radio aerial and is readily identifiable, but a stone monument which once marked the battle is broken and lost in the bush, and a quarry has disfigured part of the battlefield. The main features of the site, including the bluffs along the Thukela River where some of those fleeing the battle came to grief, are nonetheless still easy to identify. The area around the battlefield remained a strategically contested one during the Anglo-Zulu War, commanding as it did an important route between Zululand and Natal, and a bloody battle was fought over much the same ground in 1856 between two rival sons of King Mpande, the princes Cetshwayo and Mbuyazi. In 1879, the Right Flank Column of the British invading force, under Colonel C. K. Pearson, crossed the Thukela at the same drift used by the 'Grand Army of Natal' on its way to 'Ndondakusuka.

The exact site of the battle of eThaleni was only recently identified, and, taking place over a wide swathe of open country, it is not currently marked. The oPathe gorge, down which Bhongoza kaMefu led the *kommando* in December 1838, is just one of many historic sites framing the White Mfolozi river; it is close to the site of eMgungundlovu, and next to a small hill called kwaGqokli, where King Shaka won one of his first decisive battles in 1818. Across the White Mfolozi is the modern town of Ulundi, and a cluster of historic sites including King Mpande's grave, the site of King Cetshwayo's oNdini homestead, and the 1879 battlefield of Ulundi. OPathe itself is now part of a nature reserve, and the drift on the White Mfolozi where Alexander

Biggar came to grief was also the location of action during the Anglo-Zulu War – the stone remains of a small British fortification, Fort Nolela, stand close to where the regimental homestead of the uDlambedlu *ibutho* stood at the time of the battle. The field of the decisive battle of amaQongqo, the final battle of the war, is not currently marked.

Perhaps the most poignant site connected to the war is the site of King Dingane's eSankoleni homestead and his grave nearby. Situated high on the Lebombo mountains and within the Hlatikhulu Forest reserve, the very remoteness of the location is suggestive of Dingane's fall from grace. A monument on top of the hills marks the site of eSankoleni, but for many years the exact site of King Dingane's grave on the slopes beyond remained a closely-kept secret. Now it is marked by a large stone monument, but the steep track leading to it is often overgrown, and King Dingane lies in a spot that is remote even by the standard of KwaZulu Natal's historic sites. It is perhaps fitting, given his ambiguous legacy, that the king's grave is seldom visited today.

The author at King Dingane's grave at Hlatikhulu on the remote Zulu–Swazi border. In the final analysis, the king's downfall was largely the result of his own actions, which not only brought about a destructive war with the Trekkers but also a civil war within the Zulu Royal House. (Author)

FURTHER READING AND BIBLIOGRAPHY

The Voortrekker–Zulu War of 1838–40 has remained one of the most politicized in South African history. The victory of the Trekkers at Blood River/Ncome was seen by many conservative Afrikaners as a dispensation from God to rule South Africa as they saw fit, and indeed became part of the ideology of the Nationalist government during the apartheid era. In more recent times, an opposing view has emerged within Zulu nationalist historians, who dispute many key elements of the story and ascribe them to Afrikaner propaganda. Although the reign of King Dingane has been reappraised in more recent times, and the majority of interpretations occupy a more considered central ground, both extremes still exist, and literature on the wars occupies a wide spectrum in between. By far the best modern analysis, which utilizes both Afrikaner and Zulu perspectives, strips away much of the surrounding mythology and sets the war within rich layers of context, is John Laband's *The Zulu Kingdom and the Boer Invasion of 1837–40* (Warwick, 2022). A similarly scholarly study, differing in some details, is Michal Lesniewski's *The Zulu-Boer War 1837–1840* (Leiden and Boston, 2022). John Laband's *The Eight Zulu Kings: From Shaka to Goodwill Zwelithini* (Johannesburg and Cape Town, 2018) gives a good modern appraisal of King Dingane's rule. B. J. Liebenberg's *Andries Pretorius, Voortrekker Leader in Natal: Blood River to Congella, 1838–1842*, written originally in Afrikaans and translated into English by Hugh Driver (independently published, 2020), provides a thorough and demythologized biography of the great Trekker leader. Norman Etherington's *The Great Treks: The Transformation of Southern Africa 1815–1854* (Harlow, 2001) assesses the history of the Trek movements as a whole. Ian Knight's *Great Zulu Battles* (London, 1998) includes chapters on both the battles of the Thukela and Blood River/Ncome.

BIBLIOGRAPHY

Ballard, Charles, *The House of Shaka: The Zulu Monarchy Illustrated*, Durban (1988)

Becker, Peter, *Rule of Fear: The Life and Times of Dingane, King of the Zulu*, London (1964)

Chadwick, George, *The Battle of the Tugela, 17th April 1838*, National Monuments Council pamphlet, Durban (c. 1974)

Chadwick, George, *Blood River 16 December 1838*, pamphlet, Durban (1981)

Chadwick, George, *Trek Routes and Laagers in Natal*, pamphlet, Durban (1991)

Etherington, Norman, *The Great Treks: The Transformation of Southern Africa, 1815–1854*, Harlow (2001)

Gardiner, Captain Allen Francis, *Narrative of a Journey to the Zulu Country in South Africa, Undertaken in 1835*, Cape Town, reprint (1966)

Gibson, James Young, *The Story of the Zulus*, London (1911)

Knight, Ian, *The Anatomy of the Zulu Army from Shaka to Cetshwayo, 1818–1879*, London (1995)

Knight, Ian, *Great Zulu Battles*, London (1998)

Laband, John, *The Assassination of King Shaka*, Johannesburg and Cape Town (2017)

Laband, John, *The Eight Zulu Kings, from Shaka to Goodwill Zwelithini*, Johannesburg and Cape Town (2018)

Laband, John, *The Rise and Fall of the Zulu*, London (1997)

Lesniewski, Michal, *The Zulu-Boer War of 1837–40*, Leiden and Boston (2021)

Moodie, D. C. M., *The History of the Battles and Adventures of the British, The Boers, and the Zulus in Southern Africa*, Vol. 1, London (1888, reprinted 1968)

Robbertze, F. P. du P., *Die Sterfplek van Dirkie Uys*, Pietersburg (1983)

Roberts, Brian, *The Zulu Kings*, London (1974)

Rycroft, D. K. & Ngcobo, A. B. (eds), *The Praises of Dingana (Izibongo zikaDingana)*, Pietermaritzburg and Durban (1988)

Smail, J. L., *From the Land of the Zulu Kings*, Durban (1979)

Taylor, Stephen, *Shaka's Children: A History of the Zulu People*, London (1994)

Uys, Ian, *Rearguard: The Life and Times of Piet Uys*, Knysna (1998)

Walker, Eric A., *The Great Trek*, London (1938)

Webb, C. de B. & Wright, J. B. (eds), *The James Stuart Archive of Recorded Oral Evidence Relating to the History of the Zulu and neighbouring Peoples*, six volumes, Pietermaritzburg and Durban (1976, 1979, 1982, 1986, 2001, 2014)

Webb, Fleur, Alexander, Stephanie J. & Webb, Colin De B., *Adulphe Delegorgue's Travels in Southern Africa*, Vol. 1, Pietermaritzburg and Durban (1990)

INDEX

Figures in **bold** refer to illustrations.